Len Ball is in the roof slating and tiling trade, and is a founder member of the Comber Historical Society. He is also on the vestry of St. Mary's parish church, and is a former glebe warden. A keen photographer and film maker, Len has been recording everyday life in Comber since the 1960s. His interests include local railways, vintage cars and the Ards T.T.

Desmond Rainey is a civil servant and another founder member of the Comber Historical Society. He is also on the session of Second Presbyterian Church, and sings in the church choir. He has always been fascinated by history, and is a keen collector of 1960s music and old postcards.

A Taste of old Comber

The Town & its History

Len Ball & Desmond Rainey

The White Row Press

A Taste of old Comber

The Town & Its History

Len Ball & Desmond Rainey

The White Row Press

First published 2002
reprinted (without subsidy) 2003
by the White Row Press
135 Cumberland Road, Dundonald
Belfast BT16 2BB

www.whiterowpress.com

This book has received financial assistance
under the Cultural Traditions Programme

Cover: Comber Square
from the 1864 illuminated address
presented to John Andrews,
with the kind permission of Mr J. Andrews.

Printed by the Universities Press Ltd.
A catalogue record for this book is available from the British Library

ISBN 1 870132 06 8

Contents

Preface   11

1 Back to our roots   15

2 The monastic village   19

3 Two Combers   26

4 No mean village   36

5 'One shot more for the honour of Down'   45

6 Money, whiskey, linen and sweat   50

7 Railway town   63

8 Molly's world   69

9 A town mourns   81

10 Between the wars   88

11 Within living memory   99

Comber's Townlands   110

Notes   112

Bibliography   115

Index   118

To the memory of Norman Nevin, pioneer

Preface

This book is long overdue. We have been provided with several excellent local histories in recent years, among them those by Peter Carr on Dundonald and Trevor McCavery on Newtownards. So why not a book about Comber, a town that is steeped in history, right from the time of Stone Age man to the present?

The timing of the book is appropriate. First of all, Comber Historical Society, founded in 2000, has shown that there is a great interest in finding out more about our past. People are curious, for instance, as to why there is a large memorial in the Square to Sir Robert Rollo Gillespie. Who was he, they ask? Why was the Andrews Memorial Hall built? Or where was Comber railway station? Which leads on to the second point, namely the number of changes in the town within recent years. Many significant buildings have either been demolished or are earmarked for destruction. The past must be recorded before it is lost.

The authors look on this volume as a labour of love. We are mere amateurs dabbling in the world of history, although we have tried to be accurate in telling the tale. However, the book is not meant to be a detailed chronicle of every event that ever happened in the town, or a biographical dictionary of its inhabitants. Rather, we have tried to give a flavour of Comber through the ages, illustrated by pictures, many of which have not previously been published.

Much of Comber's past was researched by the late Norman Nevin MBE. Norman was not a native of Comber. He came originally from Newtownards, but settled and taught in Comber, developing a great love for the town. Over

**A MESSAGE OF LOVE.
FROM COMBER.**

This card will let you know,
That I am ever true,
But time alone can show
My wealth of love for you.

'Hoping you are well and a good boy glad to hear Aunt Aggie is a lot better'. Postcard sent to young John Niblock by his mother in 1917.

the years Norman Nevin became a well-known and popular figure here. In addition to his role as headmaster of Comber Primary School, he was Lieutenant Colonel of the army cadet force and an elder in First Comber Church. He never married, and it is said that he regarded the school as his family, maintaining an interest in his former pupils. He has been described as 'a great man with the highest morals and integrity'.

Norman Nevin passed away on 19th February 1996, just short of his eighty-seventh birthday. He left behind not only an indelible impression in people's memories, but also a wealth of information about Comber, which he meticulously studied over the years. He could often be seen about the town with his camera, recording people and events, and wrote a short unpublished history called 'The Story of Comber' which has proved invaluable to the present authors. A copy of this may be found in Comber Library, along with his collection of old photographs. In recognition of his achievement, including his influence on the present authors, we felt it only right that this book should be dedicated to his memory.

Many others must also be thanked for their assistance in the production of the book: the Comber Regeneration Group and Ards Borough Council for their keen interest and invaluable support; the Andrews family for permission to reproduce many of the pictures in this book; Aerofilms; Peter Carr for his hard work in editing the script; Ken Drain; Kathleen Coulter and the committee of Comber Historical Society; Kim Cleland for her drawing of Comber abbey; the staff at Comber, Linenhall and QUB libraries, Ordnance Survey and PRONI; Ian Wilson at the North Down Heritage Centre, Bangor; Rita Kirkpatrick and Jean Stevenson; Dave Browne; the late James Miskelly; Lester Morrow; William Robb; Erskine Willis; and all who have over the years donated the information and pictures used in this book.

Norman Nevin MBE.

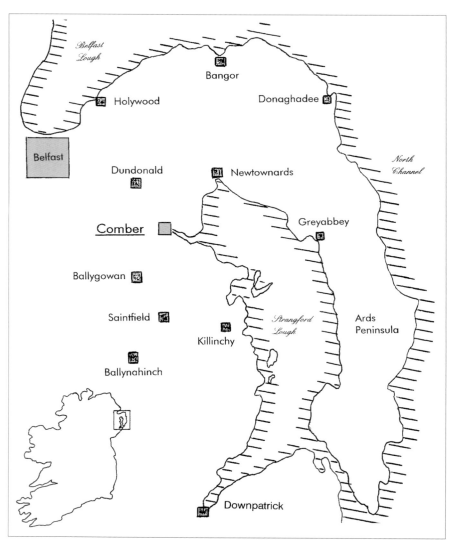

Comber, County Down, and environs.

1 Back to our roots

The little town of Comber nestles in a hollow near the estuary of the Comber River, which flows into the north-west corner of Strangford Lough. This was the strang or strong fiord of the Vikings, but it was known to the Celts by a more peaceful name – Loch Cuan, the quiet lough. It is a beautiful part of Ulster, owing much of its charm to those small rounded hills called drumlins, formed during the last Ice Age. Another legacy of the ice is the rich farmland in which the famous Comber spuds are grown. Nearby,

The Comber River from the Ballydrain Road, with Scrabo in the background.

Comber's answer to the Costa del Sol! Island Hill during its heyday. Our first ancestors made their home here some nine thousand years ago.

is the great crag and tail of Scrabo Hill, crowned by its famous nineteenth century tower built in memory of the third Marquess of Londonderry.

The Comber River is formed by the junction of the Inler[1] and Glen rivers, and this gives the town its name – the Irish word comar means the meeting place of the rivers. But, believe it or not, Comber has spent most of its life beneath the ocean waves. We know this because the sandstone and greywacke that forms much of the local bedrock was originally sand and gravel, which accumulated at the bottom of an ancient sea.

The human story of Comber, however, really begins some nine thousand years ago in the Mesolithic or Middle Stone Age, when nomadic communities lived in the Inler valley and along the shores of Strangford Lough, places well suited to their way of life. They have left behind quite a bit of evidence of their presence. For instance in 1957 two boys, Jim Swindle and Neil Witham, were clearing the new Secondary School playing fields of stones, when they stumbled on some interesting worked flints. These turned out to be Mesolithic axe heads, which are now in the Ulster Museum. And during the 1980s some two hundred worked flints were found on a low ridge by the Inler in the townland of Mount Alexander.

Flint implements are also regularly found along the beach at Island Hill. A Mesolithic midden or refuse heap was uncovered here in 1934 by archaeologists from Harvard University in the USA. This shed a fascinating light on the eating habits of our ancestors. They were hunters and gatherers, supplementing any small animals, fish, seabirds and shellfish they caught with berries, roots and nuts. These people lived close to nature, making their clothes from the skins of the animals they killed.

Around 4000 BC we enter the Neolithic or New Stone Age. New people arrived, attracted by the light soils. They had no ploughs or spades, and had to open up the ground using stakes. But first they had to clear the forests, by ring-barking or cutting down the trees with flint and stone axes. A beautiful leaf-shaped arrowhead from this period was found in 1975 by William Steele, when digging his garden on the Glen Road.

These Neolithic farmers left behind some very impressive monuments – great stone tombs, which indicate their belief in some form of afterlife. The

Dug up in a Comber garden – this beautiful Neolithic arrowhead.

The 'Five Sisters', Ballynichol.

The Five Sisters megalith on the Ballynichol Road. A huge capstone reportedly lay beside the stones in 1886. Whatever happened to it?

Bronze Age burial urn found on the site of the new Comber primary school.

dead person was going on a journey, for which he or she would need food, weapons and other items. So these were placed in the grave. The tombs are known as megaliths, from the Greek words for great stone. Several can be found around Comber, such as the Giant's Grave at Ballygraffan, and the Five Sisters on the Ballynichol Road. In 1887 Bassett mentions that there was a prostrate capstone eighteen feet long, five feet broad and four feet thick lying beside the Five Sisters. This dolmen, described by Bassett as a Druid's Altar, had been used by Roman Catholics as a place of worship in the days when the celebration of the mass was forbidden. It has now disappeared, and one can only wonder at how such a gigantic stone could simply vanish into thin air! Indeed, it is a mystery how stones weighing above twenty tons could have been erected in the first place with not an excavator, crane or lowloader in sight.

Around 2500-2000 BC people discovered minerals in the earth. These could be melted and mixed together to produce a strong material, for instance copper and tin, used in the proportion of one part tin to nine parts copper formed bronze. Hence the Bronze Age. By 1750 BC a thriving bronze industry had been established. One very notable local Bronze Age settlement site has survived – right in the middle of the golf course on Scrabo. Or should we call it Scraba, as it was known in bygone days? Scraba or scrath-ba would mean 'the rough ground', while Scrabo is 'the sward of the cows'. Take your pick. Several cists or stone-lined graves from the period have been found around Comber. The first was discovered in 1850 near the Andrews' bleach green (now the cricket ground). Similar finds occurred in 1858 beside the Inler near what is now the car park, in 1885 at Ballyloughan (between Comber and Ballystockart), and in 1937 on the site of the new Primary School on the Darragh Road.

By around 300 BC the Celts had arrived and were using iron. The geographer Ptolemy places a tribe called the Darini in North Down in the second century AD. They would have been part of the kingdom of the Ulaid (Ulster). You may have paid a visit to what was then its capital – Emain Macha (Navan Fort outside Armagh).

2 The monastic village

egend has it that Christianity came to Comber with St. Patrick. He did not receive a particularly warm welcome. Indeed we read of him being 'sorely abused' by Saran, a son of the local chieftain. Saran's brother Conla, however, was more hospitable. He apologised to the saint and offered him a field called the 'Plain of Elom' on which to build a church. And so Comber got its first monastery. It may have been near the cricket green. In fact a lane

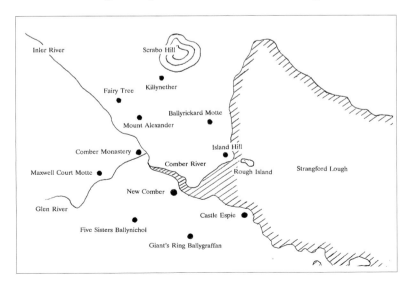

Early sites and antiquities in the Comber area.

The ruined round tower at Nendrum, once mistaken for a lime kiln. It failed to protect abbot Sedna O'Denman, who was burned here in 974.

running from what is now the car park towards Castle Lane was once known as the Monks' Walk, which would seem to preserve the remnant of some ancient memory.

Comber was part of a network of Celtic monasteries in the area. Another was Nendrum, the ruins of which can be seen on Mahee Island, named after its founder, St. Mochaoi. This was an ideal site for a lonely life of contemplation. The island has only recently been connected to the mainland by a causeway. Nendrum was extensively excavated in 1922-24, but the site had actually been lost until 1844, when the antiquarian bishop William Reeves was shown an old lime kiln, which turned out to be something quite different – the stump of the monastery's round tower! This probably stood some sixty feet (eighteen metres) high, a place of refuge from the Vikings and other raiders, who saw the rich monasteries as easy pickings. However, it didn't save the skin of the abbot Sedna O'Denman who was 'burned in his own home' by the Vikings in the year 974.

The monastery bell, used for calling the monks to prayer, disappeared at around the same time. Imagine the amazement of the archaeologists some 950 years later when they found it staring at them from the hole in the ground in which the monks had hidden it! Today it rests in the Ulster Museum.

Nendrum's sundial also survives, propped up against the wall of its old stone church. It surely couldn't have been much use in our dull climate. The monastery is still yielding up its secrets. Great excitement has recently been caused by the discovery of the tidal mill in which the monks ground their corn. A fragment of its timber has been dated to the year 620.

Kill Combuir (the church of Comber) suffered the same fate as Nendrum in 1031, when Vikings killed four clerics and carried off thirty as captives. In another raid in 1121 the death is recorded of Cormac, abbot of Comar. By this stage Comber was occupied by the Augustinians, and was known as the Black Abbey due to the colour of habit worn by its monks.

In 1177 the Normans, under John de Courcy, conquered eastern County Down. De Courcy rewarded his victorious knights with large estates. The Comber district went to Ralph de Rossal. In order to secure the region, a network of forts or mottes was constructed. These mottes were raised mounds of earth, surmounted by a palisade or perhaps a small wooden keep. Traces of mottes can be found at Maxwell Court on the Ballygowan Road, just

e motte at Maxwell Court. e field gate (centre) conveys e scale.

outside Comber, and at the Moate Corner between Comber and Newtownards. The land was divided into bailiwicks, the Norman equivalent of our modern baronies. In 1226 five of these are recorded – Comber lay in the bailiwick of Blathewic.

The Normans were great church builders. De Courcy repaired Nendrum, which was re-settled by the Benedictines, and his wife Affreca established a Cistercian abbey at Greyabbey. In 1199 a similar abbey was founded at Comber on land donated by the local magnate, Brian Catha Dun. If Brian made the grant in order to win the favour of the lord of Ulster, then it got him nowhere, for by 1201 he lay dead after getting on the wrong side of de Courcy.

The building of the new abbey was an enormous event in medieval

Artist's impression of Comber's Cistercian monastery in its prime. St. Mary's now occupies the site. The modern Square was at the top of the drawing. The Cistercians were known as 'the White Monks' from the colour of their habit.

Comber's history. Masons who had worked on Greyabbey now came to work on Comber. We know this because stones with identical mason's marks have been discovered at both sites. The Comber stone has, unfortunately, disappeared. Monks from Albalanda in Carmarthenshire were brought over to staff the new abbey, which was roughly on the site today occupied by St. Mary's Church of Ireland. Although all trace of it has now gone, many stones from the ruins were re-used in walls and buildings around the present church.

Comber Abbey must have been very similar to Greyabbey, as Cistercian abbeys, rather like McDonald's burger bars in our own time, were built to a standard layout prescribed by the Order. The abbey would have been very imposing. A visit to the ruins at Greyabbey will reveal the magnitude of the structure which once proudly stood near Comber Square. Part – and maybe most – of the Square was then a burial ground associated with the monastery. We know this because human bones were unearthed here in 1844 when the foundations of the Gillespie monument were being dug. So a place today full of traffic and bustle was once a quiet sacred space. Traces of what may have been a medieval drainage system were found in a bed of smooth damp

These curious hewn stones lie in a garden near the Square. They are said to have come from the abbey. Note the carved head. Could this be an abbot?

clay. It appeared to have flowed from the Glen River, beside the Upper Distillery, into the Inler behind the houses in Bridge Street. The monastery seems to have had every medieval mod con, including a sanitation system that incorporated a crude type of flush toilet!

The arrival of the Norman abbey cannot, however, have been good news for the Augustinian Black Abbey. Its history now becomes obscure and we can only guess at its fate. Traces of its buildings survived until 1644. As it declined, the new abbey flourished, becoming rich and important. The presence of Andrew, abbot of Cummor, is recorded at Bangor in 1251.

Many smaller churches also existed, of which there is now no trace. One such was Ballyrickard, opposite the motte on the road to Scrabo. It was described as ruinous in 1622. O'Laverty mentions the site of another church in the townland of Castlebeg, on the Belfast Road. Graves were uncovered here around 1830 in a field known as the Fairy Field. Until the 1950s the traditional church site was marked by a ring of boulders, the Fairy Ring, where the fairies were said to dance. Today a lone sycamore tree marks the spot. And if you wanted cured of warts, you could visit the ancient well at Killynether. Close by stood a rude, chair-shaped stone, said to be where a holy man called Old Cowey used to come and pray. The present authors have been unable to identify this stone.

In the 1200s the monastery and the Norman colony flourished. In 1315 however, the peace of the district was shattered when Edward, brother of the Scots king Robert Bruce, invaded Ireland, causing devastation. The fourteenth century was also plagued by a series of bad harvests and famines. Add to this the Black Death of 1348 and we are left with the impression of a struggling, underpopulated settlement that was unable to attract new people or properly defend its borders.

By the mid-fifteenth century the Norman presence had greatly weakened, allowing North Down to pass into the hands of the O'Neills of Claneboye. This was the era when the upper classes lived in so-called tower houses, such as that at Sketrick near Killinchy, probably built by the De Mandevilles. Its capture by Henry O'Neill in 1470 is recorded. And in 1536 we find the use of artillery in Ireland first mentioned here. Sketrick fell into a ruinous condition over the years, and what remained was shattered by a thunderstorm in 1896.

North Down c. 1580, with north oriented to the right. 'Conner' is the modern Comber. The abbeys of Newtownards, Bangor and Greyabbey are also marked, as is Sketrick (Skyrik).

Comber monastery lasted until 1543, when it was closed by Henry VIII, along with all the other religious foundations in the country. Its wealth and lands passed to the king, the last abbot, John O'Mullegan, being deprived of seven townlands, as well as other dependencies.

A succession of English adventurers then pressed Henry's daughter, Queen Elizabeth I, for territory in North Down. One of these, a Captain Browne, is said to have built the tower house on Mahee Island in 1570, the ruins of which are still to be seen. The chief of Claneboye, Bryan McPhelim O'Neill, described as a 'true subject' in government papers, was furious when the queen gave his lands to Sir Thomas Smith in 1571. Smith's son, also Thomas, arrived on the shores of Strangford Lough to stake his father's claim, but O'Neill wasn't going to lie down without a fight. He fought a guerrilla war, laying waste the countryside to deprive the English of food and shelter. Among buildings put to the torch was the ancient abbey of Comber. Young Smith did succeed in establishing a base at Comber, but he was murdered here in 1573 by an Irish retainer.

The Earl of Essex now comes swaggering on to the scene. He defeated O'Neill, putting him to death in rather treacherous circumstances. By 1603 the power of the O'Neills was broken. However it was not the English, but the Scots, who would inherit the spoils.

3 Two Combers

At the time of Queen Elizabeth's death, the lord of Claneboye, Con O'Neill, lay languishing in the gaol of Carrickfergus Castle. His prospects looked grim until a canny Scotsman made a bargain with him. This was Hugh Montgomery, laird of Braidstane in Ayrshire, who enjoyed the favour of the new king, James I. Montgomery promised to arrange Con's escape and pardon in return for half his lands. And he did. But there was another vulture circling, a second native of Ayrshire, called James Hamilton. He persuaded the king to let him in on the act, with the result that the territories of poor O'Neill were divided into three portions. The parish of Comber was split, with approximately two-thirds going to Montgomery and one-third to Hamilton.

Hugh Montgomery arrived in 1606, and the new settlers proceeded to build homes in what seems to have been a largely wasted countryside. By 1611 Lady Montgomery had a farm at 'Comar', and it is interesting to see that the earliest authenticated reference to potatoes in Ireland occurs here in 1606. Around 1610 a portion of Comber's by now ruined abbey was fitted out as a church, with Hugh Montgomery paying two-thirds and Sir James Hamilton, soon to become Viscount Claneboye, paying for one-third of the rebuilding. Hugh Montgomery was episcopalian in his religious views: that is to say he believed in the rule of bishops. All 'his' clergy had to share these views, including, we must assume, James Fresall, who was appointed minister in 1622, and about whom we know absolutely nothing.

In the 1830s the old church was described as having '…no tower or steeple. It is built like a common house with merely a small arch erected on its southern

The mighty fallen. Mount Alexander, complete with slurry tank. Once a home fit for an earl.

gable, in which is a bell'. Montgomery, created a viscount in 1622, supplied a bell and a Geneva or 'Breeches' bible to each of the churches on his estate. Bells were very necessary items in the days when few people possessed a clock. Unfortunately the original Comber bell was lost in 1641.

Many of the Scots settlers found their last resting-place in St. Mary's churchyard, where several early tombstones can be found. One interesting headstone, today reposing against the wall of the church, is that of Isaac Meredith of Kilbreght. He died in 1723 and was believed to have reached the grand old age of 127! Perhaps he just lost count of the years. Or has someone rather mischievously inserted an extra digit? Two other stones are embedded within the interior of the church tower. The dates inscribed on these enigmatic tablets are 1633 and 1637, marking them out as the earliest known remains relating to the church of the settlers.

In 1622 Montgomery's eldest son, also Hugh, married Lady Jean Alexander, daughter of the Secretary for Scotland. As a wedding present Sir Hugh built a large house for the couple on a gently rising hill outside Comber, which he called Mount Alexander Castle. The stone for the building came from the abandoned Cistercian Abbey. This house has now disappeared, apart from a section of wall supporting a hay shed. Its name lives on, however, in Castle Lane, which runs by where it stood. Close by was the Kennel Bridge, named after the kennels where the hunting hounds were kept. This

Hoping for a bite at the old five-arch Kennel Bridge, demolished in 1995.

fine old bridge, a popular spot for fishing, was demolished and replaced in 1995 by an award-winning, single arched structure, which incorporates one of the original stones, a stone that bears a mason's mark.

Not to be outdone, Sir James Hamilton built a completely new village in his part of the parish, on what is now the Ballydrain Road. This became known as New Comber, as opposed to Owld Comber for the original settlement around the abbey. The name is still retained in New Comber Bridge and New Comber House. Hamilton's 'rival' village was a considerable settlement. A map, made by Thomas Raven in 1625, shows forty-two detached cottages, laid out in one main street and two side streets. This would have made it one of the largest villages in Ulster, with almost as many houses as a town such as Holywood. Bangor had some eighty houses at the time, while Montgomery's Newtownards had around one hundred. Each cottage had a long strip of land for growing vegetables. North of the bridge is a square, containing a mercat (or market) cross. On the south side of the village was a ball green, on which stood what looks like either a maypole or gibbet. The residence of Robert Hamilton, nephew of Lord Claneboye, is marked. That Hamilton should settle his nephew here is a clear sign of his commitment to

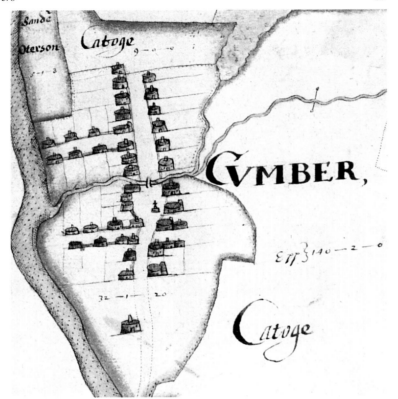

The competition. 'New Comber', from the 1625 Raven maps. Strangely enough, south is to the top. Note the 'mercat cross'.

the place. Hamilton was determined to make his wing of the parish burgeon. We know almost nothing more about this interesting but doomed settlement. When Owld Comber was relaunched in 1731, New Comber declined and in time ceased to exist.

Both Combers were shaken to their foundations by the rebellion of 1641. Hugh Montgomery had died in 1636, and two Comber men, Thomas Kennedy and John Lockart, led his funeral procession. It was therefore left to his son Hugh, the second viscount, to look to the defence of his tenants. He received a commission as colonel, and authority to muster one thousand foot and five troops of horse, which he paid for. Hamilton, now in his eighties, also raised a regiment. In February 1642 Comber came

Worshippers gather at First Comber Presbyterian Church in 1864. The present church is scarcely recognisable from this structure. Note the outside steps leading up to a gallery. These were removed in 1887.

under attack. The Irish swept up from Killinchy to within a mile of the town. Here, at a place named as Battletown (site now unknown) by the author of the *Montgomery Manuscripts*, they met with strenuous opposition and were put to flight.

With the arrival of a Scots army in 1642, the balance of power swung in favour of the settlers. Presbyterianism, long latent in the Ulster colony, also received a boost when five army chaplains formed a Presbytery and took measures to reorganise the church in Ireland. Applications for ministers were received from many parishes, of which Comber was one. And so in 1645 James Gordon arrived as a Presbyterian minister, mainly through the influence of Lady Jean, widow of the second Viscount Montgomery, who had died in 1642 of a 'drowsy distemper'.

The position of these early ministers was peculiar. Although Presbyterian in doctrine, they were admitted by bishops to the episcopalian churches and received tithes. And so, although the Presbyterian congregation of First Comber dates itself from Gordon's arrival, strictly speaking, he was minister of St. Mary's. In 1657 he is reported as a preacher in salary, with a dwelling house and six acres of land. But relations with the Montgomerys became strained. In 1649, for instance, Gordon refused to baptise the third viscount's daughter unless he stood on the penitential stool and denied episcopalian doctrine. Montgomery refused, and so another minister had to be found for the baptism.[1]

When James Hamilton passed away in 1643, his son, also James, was raised to the peerage as Earl of Clanbrassil. Both Montgomery and Clanbrassil supported the king during the Civil War. The king lost, as a result of which both men suffered greatly. Montgomery was imprisoned in 1646, but later took up arms again as general of the royalist forces in Ulster. Both he and Clanbrassil submitted to Oliver Cromwell in 1649. Clanbrassil forfeited his estates pending payment of a huge fine. His wife secured her husband's release, and eventually the return of his estates. But his spirit had been broken, and he died in 1659. Montgomery was banished to Holland, but later allowed back on payment of a fine. After his young wife died in 1655 his health deteriorated and he returned to live with his mother at Mount Alexander.

Montgomery's troubles ended with the restoration of Charles II in 1660. He was created Earl of Mount Alexander and, after three short years of happiness, died in 1663. His son fell into debt and sold off the Montgomery estates. By 1679 most of the estate of Mount Alexander had been knocked down to Sir Robert Colvil for the sum of £9,780. What remained went to Montgomery's brother Henry in 1716. He devoted himself to farming until his death in 1731. His sons Hugh and Thomas became fourth and fifth earls, until in 1760 the Montgomery line came to an end.

The Scots in Ireland had hoped that Charles II would support the Presbyterian Church. However, they were to be disappointed. Charles re-established the bishops, and Jeremy Taylor, Bishop of Down, gave ministers the choice of either conforming or being thrown out. James Gordon of Comber was one of those expelled. In 1663 he was imprisoned, having been implicated in a plot to restore the Commonwealth. There was no evidence against him or indeed any trial, but he was given the choice of staying in prison or leaving the kingdom. Lady Montgomery interceded on Gordon's behalf, and he was allowed to return to Comber. But not as minister. His place had been taken by William Dowdall in 1661. Dowdall met with much opposition, especially from women who attacked him in the church and pulled off his surplice. At their trial in Downpatrick one of the rioters boastfully informed the judge, 'These are the hauns that poo'd the white sark ower his heed'. Gordon took charge of the large Presbyterian congregation in Comber, while Dowdall remained as Church of Ireland minister until 1692.

'Affable, courteous and complacent.' Henry, third earl of Mount Alexander, who came back to live in Comber in 1716.

Today, First Comber Presbyterian Church sits proudly at the top of High Street, the Coo Vennel or Cow Lane of the Scots settlers. The first meeting house was probably erected around 1670. The lease of the present church dates from 1686, during the ministry of John Hamilton. The original building was a low thatched affair, whitewashed inside and out, with no pews. During worship the men generally stood, although women could bring stools – and this at a time when the sermon could last for hours! A school was established about 1685. It closed during the Williamite wars and never re-opened.

On 3rd December 1688 an anonymous letter was found in the streets of Comber, addressed to the Earl of Mount Alexander, warning of an imminent massacre of protestants. The letter caused panic, and set in motion a sequence of events which led to the shutting of the gates of Derry. All or most of Comber's bigwigs fled the parish – John Hamilton, the Presbyterian minister; John Binning the schoolmaster; Sir Robert Colvil who had bought the Comber

Orangeman James Brown with a fascinating relic from the Boyne campaign. King William is said to have been treated on this chair in 1690. It now resides in Comber Orange Hall.

estate; Thomas Herington and his son, both large landowners; and John Griffith, also from Comber.

The Jacobite army occupied the region and religious services were suspended. During these troubled times the Reverend Gilbert Kennedy of Dundonald is said to have preached in the glens near Comber. In August 1689 Schomberg's army brought relief. Now King William's men were in the ascendant. We have a relic from the Williamite Wars in Comber Orange Hall. This is a chair which originally belonged to Surgeon Sandford, an officer in William's army. Good King Billy is said to have been medically treated on this chair on his march to the Boyne.

The district recovered slowly from the upset of the wars. The town's ministers provided leadership. The then rector, Edmund Bennett, is described on a stone inscription outside the church as a 'learned and pious minister', who on his death in 1710 was 'very much lamented'.

Comber was an overwhelmingly Presbyterian parish, so the arrival of a new Presbyterian minister was a big event. In 1724 John Orr was installed. He was a non-subscriber, that is to say he refused to subscribe to the Westminster Confession of Faith. When they learned this, many members of Orr's congregation were outraged. They tried to bar him from the meeting house, and this led to forty-nine persons being charged with taking forcible possession of the church and refusing the minister access. Desperate times called for desperate measures. In an attempt to make the occupation lawful, a local octogenarian called James Maxwell performed the amazing feat of riding to Dublin to obtain a legal instrument against Orr, returning the next day and delivering it to the High Sheriff. The case went to trial. The judge took a dim view of Orr, describing him as 'more like a wolf or tyrant to conspire against the people as he had done'. Orr left, eventually to join the Church of Ireland where he flourished, becoming Dean of Raphoe.

After much politicking and manoeuvring, Robert Cunningham was ordained as Orr's successor in 1728. During his time the meeting house was extended. A stone found some years ago in an out-house of the manse celebrates this extension: 'This House was built in the year 1740. The Rev. Robert Cunningham, Minister'. It was placed in a wall of the church. It was reported at that time that there were only two slated houses in the parish – the Glebe and Ballybeen House, so the new meeting house was probably

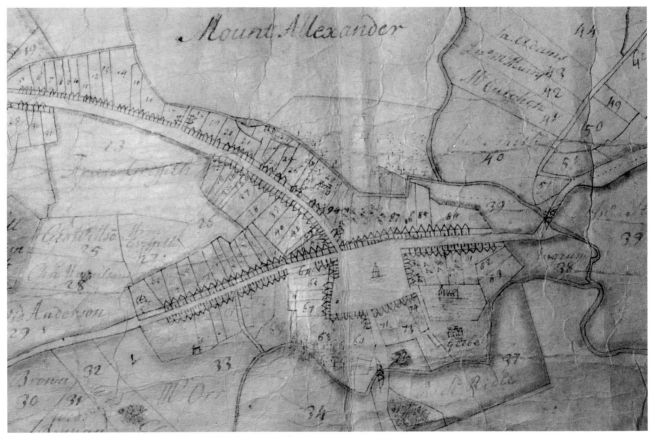

thatched. Cunningham retired in 1772 due to infirmity.

He would have had a busy ministry. In 1764 there were 1,220 Presbyterians, as opposed to 315 members of the established church, and 165 'papists' in the parish. These figures come from a census completed by an excise officer or 'gauger'. Excise officers supervised trading and tax collection in Strangford Lough, where the smuggling of items such as rum, wine, sugar, tea and whiskey was commonplace. The Ghaist Hole on the Killinchy Road was a favourite spot for landing these illicit cargoes, and it is said that the smugglers suspended a white sheet over the road to frighten

Comber in 1722, showing the predecessor of the modern Square with its 'mercat cross'. The street pattern is already familiar, but note the position of Killinchy Street, about halfway along the southern side of the Square. The Square was revamped in 1731, leading to the demolition of many old buildings.

The 'ghaist' hole on the Killinchy Road, once the haunt of smugglers. They scared off intruders using a white sheet, hence the 'ghaist' or ghost. Today this is the home of the local cruising club, also known as the 'Comber Navy'.

passers by. This was the ghaist or ghost.

Errant Presbyterians appeared before the Kirk Session, a court of morals. It heard cases dealing with misdemeanours such as adultery, drunkenness, the taking of the Lord's name in vain and scolding wives! The responsibilities of Comber parish church, however, were more than simply congregational. The parish was the unit of local government. Comber parish is made up of forty-five townlands, which makes it quite a large unit. The parish vestry supervised the collection of the 'cess', a local tax, set in 1720 at ten guineas. The money raised was largely spent on maintaining the roads, and much of the vestry's efforts were pitched in this direction. For instance in 1737 it was enacted 'that 5 shill be laid on ye town of Cumber for picks for ye highways', and in 1744 it was 'further enacted yt Sam Breadly be made Survr (surveyor) for st field (Saintfield) road'.

The vestry also dutifully attended to minor matters, such as 'washing the (parish) linen', 'stopping up the little window' and 'making the cushion', as well as the purchase of a surplice and two books of homilies. And in 1732 the sexton was given $6\frac{1}{2}$d to equip the church bell with cords. But the vestry was also concerned with helping the poor. There was, for instance, payment of two pounds to Andrew McBurney for 'maintaining ye bastard' in 1728. In the same year $2/8\frac{1}{2}$d was allocated to the woman 'that nursed the poor child'. Unfortunately the child died, whereon tenpence was given out for 'pipes and tobacco at the poor child's funeral'.

4 No mean village

In 1744 Walter Harris published *The Antient and Present State of the County of Down*. He does not have much good to say about Comber:

Comber is but a mean village, and has no trade; yet seems by its situation to be capable of it, on account of the advantages of the tide. There is here at low water a pleasant strand of some thousands of acres, and near the town a horse-course of a noted fine sod two miles in circuit... There is now in the town a large meeting house, and a decent church, with a vicarage house.

It seems rather unfair to call our lovely little town a mean village, but no doubt Mr Harris had his reasons. Indeed we should probably look sympathetically at his comments because he did see a potential for growth.

Parish Church and Glebe House.

The glebe house (r), built in 1738 for the rector of St. Mary's. The present church dates from 1840. To the left can be seen the large burial vault of the Andrews family.

'Allo, 'allo. Constable Jim McNish looks for traffic to direct in a rather deserted looking Square in the 1920s-30s. The two sentry box doorways on the Georgian houses behind him are original features.

Comber had in fact been extensively re-planned in 1731, and the town's fine Georgian Square dates from this time. Several superb early Georgian houses can still be seen here, with their distinctive windows, and 'sentry-box' doorways. The racecourse referred to by Harris was at Cherryvalley, and a hill there is still called Racecourse Hill. The Vicarage or Glebe House had been built in 1738 beside the Church of Ireland (the 'decent church' of Harris' account). It was demolished in 1958.

Soon afterwards the town of Comber underwent another change of ownership. Alexander Stewart, father of the first Lord Londonderry, purchased Comber from the Colvils in 1744. But it was another family, the Andrews', who were largely responsible for transforming Harris' mean little village into the hive of industry that he saw it could become. The Andrews had arrived in Ulster from Scotland in the early seventeenth century, apparently settling on Mahee Island, and living there until at least 1630.[1]

The Andrews family made their money in milling. In the late seventeenth century Comber had two corn mills. Both fell into the hands of Thomas Andrew (1698–1743), who in 1735 changed the family name to Andrews, to

A horse and carriage drives past John Andrews' house in Castle Street (the Old House) in 1864. Some very natty locals look on. Comber was far from being as affluent as this picture suggests.

distinguish himself from Thomas Andrew the cooper, a distant cousin.[2] After his death his sons John (1721–1808) and Thomas (b.1727) carried on the family business. At the time of his father's death John was living in Belfast, where he seems to have been apprenticed to the linen trade, and it took him a while to decide to return to Comber. When he came back in 1745, one of his first acts was to build a house for himself in Castle Street. This became fondly known as the Old House. It is now the site of the Supervalu supermarket. In 1746 John brought his new wife, Mary Corbitt, to live here. His brother Thomas did not remain in Comber. He rented a bleach green in Ballymena and in 1774 went to Jamaica, where he ended his days a very wealthy man.[3] It was left to John to expand the Andrews' enterprises in Comber, which he did with a vengeance, truly deserving his nickname of 'John the Great'.

Diversification was perhaps the secret of John's success. As well as working the corn mills, he made soap and candles at a site in Castle Street. The candles had the trade name of 'Watchlights'. For some unknown reason candle making stopped in 1785, and soap boiling in 1788. Thomas's departure may have been a reason for this pruning. In any case, John had more than enough to keep himself occupied. In 1745 he had established a wash mill and bleach green on what are now the grounds of North Down Cricket Club. This enterprise flourished, and in 1763 two thousand pieces of linen were bleached. In the 1770s he rebuilt the entire works and erected a beetling mill so that he could add further value to his linen produce by flattening the

'John the great' (1721-1808), who turned Walter Harris' 'mean little village' into an industrial town.

fabric. Fortune seems to have smiled on John. In 1783 he even won ten thousand pounds on the Irish State Lottery, and purchased the townland of Carnesure with his winnings.

Andrews was a natural entrepreneur, always on the lookout for a business opportunity. When, after food shortages, Parliament offered bounties to develop flour milling, John Andrews caught the wave, building a massive five-storey flour mill in 1771, at a cost of £1,400. This was another success for the firm, and the building remained as a landmark in Comber until around 1900. Wheat was collected in all the little ports on Strangford Lough and shipped in small vessels to the mouth of the Comber River, where it was unloaded at Ringcreevy and carted to the mill. Cargoes also arrived from Dublin or Drogheda, and even the North American colonies.

Stone was quarried from what is now the site of the Baptist church. This was used for building and on the roads. Every man was required to give his own labour and the work of a horse for six days in the year, making and

Industrial might and architectural pretensions. The 1771 flour mill. Note the cupola with what looks like a weather vane on top. In the right background is the equally enormous grain store of 1863. Industrially, our little town punched well above its weight.

repairing roads, although the better off paid others to do the work for them. John Andrews built Mill Street and the Pound Bridge. The Pound (an enclosure for stray animals, redeemable by their owners on payment of a fee to the authorities) occupied the site of Thompson's dance hall, later the Technical School, recently demolished.

The beauties of Castle Street. View from the gateway of the Old House to James Andrews' house, Uraghamore. In the 1830s this was one of only two three-storey houses in Comber, the other being the Stitt family home in the Square, later Kane's showrooms. In the left background is one of Uraghamore's ancient yews.

John Wesley, founder of Methodism, who visited Comber in 1758.

Comber seems to have had quite a lively social life. For instance in 1763 a Mr. Vincent advertised singing lessons, suggesting a certain amount of wealth and gentility in the town and surrounding countryside. In the same year we read of a charity ball held at Mount Alexander Castle for the benefit of a family in distress. Tickets, at 2/2d each, could be obtained at Mr. Alexander Riddle's, a merchant in Comber. And in 1795 the *Northern Star* announced a meeting of the 'Comber coterie', which would seem to have been a literary or perhaps political debating club. However not everyone could afford to apply themselves to such abstracts. In 1760 a labourers' pay was a mere eight pence per day. Out of this he had to feed himself and his family, as well as rent a cottage and small piece of land on which to grow potatoes and vegetables, and perhaps graze a cow. With holdings like this renting at some thirty shillings a year, he would have had little left over in his pocket.

In 1758 Comber also received a visit from John Wesley, the founder of Methodism. He returned on two further occasions. On his 1760 visit he began to preach as soon as the normal church service was over. We are told that four in five of the audience behaved well, which is good going, considering that Wesley's preaching often prompted rioting. Not withstanding intense opposition from the local ministers, Wesley won a small but dedicated band of followers. The Presbyterian minister Robert Cunningham initially expelled the Methodist defectors from the Lord's table, but later sent his elders to invite them back. However, the growth of the new church in Comber was checked in 1766 when two of its leaders died in quick succession, and a prominent member, in whose house the society met, was expelled. Methodists continued to meet in private houses until 1820, when they built their own 'mission station' in Newtown Street, now Bridge Street.

By 1786 Comber had a post office, showing that the town had made advances. However it had not quite attained civilisation. In the same year John Andrews' son, James, was robbed by footpads on his way home from Belfast. James was twenty-four at the time and stood six feet four inches tall. As the Andrews' heir, James was the coming man. At the time of his marriage to Frances Glenny in 1792 he built a stylish house just across the street from the Old House. He called it Uraghamore, 'place of the big yew trees'. It was latterly the Comber Sports Centre. These trees were believed to be at least four hundred years old. The garden was on a steep incline, set out in three levels, fenced off from the street by a wall surmounted by an iron railing. It was known locally as the Palace Stages.

In 1775 Britain went to war against its former American colonies. France joined in, and in 1778 companies of Volunteers were formed to defend the nation. There were two in Comber, one commanded by John Andrews and the other by Robert Stewart, afterwards the first Lord Londonderry. In 1779, Stewart was promoted to colonel and Hugh Gillespie took his place. John Andrews' company, the Comber Rangers, was raised entirely by himself. Its uniform was red with green facings. Many of its members were employees of their captain.

The 1783 election raised high passion in the town and district. Most of the Volunteers supported the liberal candidate, who was none other than their old captain Robert Stewart. His successor Hugh Gillespie, however, actively supported the opposition. Maybe over actively. Stewart's faction accused him of using 'unconstitutional means…to induce freeholders to vote contrary to their inclinations'. This cost him his position, and he was rejected by his company, being replaced by Robert Rollo Reid. The company now took the name of the Comber True Blues. Gillespie denied the charges, and the matter was only resolved in June 1784, when Andrews and Gillespie duelled at a spot described as being near 'the Mall', location unknown. Both men missed, whereupon their seconds intervened and the matter was honourably settled. The Volunteers were disbanded in 1793.

This was the time of the United Irishmen, founded in 1791 to push for reform of parliament and repeal of the penal laws. Most of the principal inhabitants of Comber joined. But when the Society began to develop a revolutionary ethos, propertied members, such as John Andrews, withdrew. These were turbulent times. In March 1797 a number of men beset Unicarval House outside Comber, the home of Mr. Cuming, a respectable farmer, demanding any weapons that he had. He fired at them, whereupon they broke in and murdered him. Shortly afterwards County Down was put under martial law. This led to many atrocities on the part of the soldiers, particularly the York Fencibles. Soldiers quartered in Comber during the next two years burned many houses of suspected United Irishmen.

Talk of rebellion was in the air, a rebellion towards which the Presbyterians

James Andrews (1762-1841) in his Volunteer uniform. James stood 6'4", and it is said that an ordinary man with his shoes on could put his feet inside James' shoes.

Pike head discovered in the thatch of a cottage near Island Hill. Note the extensive signs of use around the tip. Did it spill blood in 1798?

of Comber were generally sympathetic. Pikes by the hundred were secretly made at dead of night in the local blacksmiths' shops. A pike had a long wooden shaft, attached to a pointed metal head about ten inches (25 cm) long. In recent years a pike head was found in the thatch of an old cottage being pulled down at Island Hill, where it may have been hidden in 1798. Muskets were smuggled in at the Ghaist Hole. Other weapons were – very daringly – pilfered from the soldiers, as witnessed by the following snippet from the *Northern Star* in 1796:

A few days ago the arms and accoutrements of a small company of dragoons were stolen out of the stable of Mr Barns of Comber where they were quartered.

On Saturday 9th June 1798 the rebels assembled on Scrabo Hill, and passed through Comber on their way to Saintfield. They were pursued by Colonel Stapleton and the York Fencibles, along with the Newtownards and Comber Yeomanry, and two pieces of cannon. The soldiers were accompanied by the rector of Comber, the Rev. Robert Mortimer, and his nephew. Stapleton's men were ambushed outside Saintfield, and returned to Comber in disarray, quartering themselves in the Presbyterian meeting house. The Mortimers did not return with them. They had perished at Saintfield. Their bodies most likely rest in a mass grave at a place still known as York Island, because most of the dead belonged to the York Fencibles. St. Mary's Church of Ireland has a memorial to another three men who didn't come back. This tablet commemorates Captain Unit, Lieutenant Chetwynd and Ensign Sparks, and is the only memorial in the province dedicated to regular government troops.

The 1798 Rebellion in County Down ended with a government victory at Ballynahinch. The aftermath was bloody, but Comber seems to have escaped lightly. The only recorded casualty came in October, when a person named Clarke was hanged in the Square, and his head placed upon a spike. A few years ago workmen came upon an oak beam in perfect condition about four feet (1.2 metres) below the surface in the Square. It had been sawn off and was sunk into the ground. Was this the remains of the gibbet?

5 'One shot more for the honour of Down'

Today visitors to Comber inevitably gravitate towards the town's Georgian Square. And there right in the middle, towering above the Memorial Gardens, is a fifty-five foot (seventeen metre) high column surmounted by the statue of Comber's most famous son. This is none other than Sir Robert Rollo Gillespie, who fought in the armies of King George III, and became a legend in his own lifetime. Many an unsuspecting novice policeman in the town, when asking for a wrongdoer's address, was given the answer – 'Gillespie, the Square'. He didn't usually make the same mistake again.

Gillespie's grandfather had come over from Scotland and built a large house at Cherryvalley outside Comber. Robert spent his early years there. But he was actually born in a cousin's house in the Square in 1766. This house was knocked down some time after 1844. Rumour has it that a hoard of gold was found by the demolition squad. According to legend, they never worked again!

We like to think of Gillespie as a Comber man, but he really spent very little time here. Before he was ten years old his parents moved to the fashionable spa town of Bath, and so Gillespie spent his youth and received his education in England. He always wanted to be a soldier and persuaded his parents to let him enter the cavalry as a cornet. He led a boisterous, bachelor lifestyle until he became entranced with a Dublin girl called Annabella Taylor. In 1786 the pair eloped and were married.

Soon afterwards Gillespie was involved in a duel in County Kildare. He was second to a fellow officer who was fighting a local squire called William

Sir Robert Rollo Gillespie (1766-1814).

Barrington. But things got rather out of hand, and it was Gillespie who ended up shooting and killing Barrington! Gillespie fled. But to his credit he returned to face the music, and somehow or other managed to get acquitted.

In 1792 our hero, now a lieutenant in the Twentieth Light Dragoons, set sail for the West Indies to fight the French. Two years later, after being promoted to captain, Gillespie took part in an attack on the French-held fort at Tiburon. He led his men up the hilly path to the fort in the dark and surprised its occupants, capturing the bastion. Gillespie and a colleague now volunteered to carry a summons of surrender to the French at Port-au-Prince. But they were captured and taken before the governor, charged with spying. The situation was serious. Now Gillespie was a freemason, and by good fortune so was the governor. All ended up the best of friends, although the French didn't surrender.

Gillespie was very patriotic. In 1796 he was in Cork waiting to return to

The Illustrated London News *shows the alleged thirty thousand who packed the Square for the unveiling of the Gillespie monument. It looks like the Twelfth of July with all those flags, but the only band playing was the Newtownards Amateur Band, seen in the foreground. Note the Erasmus Smith schoolhouse to the left of St. Mary's.*

the West Indies. At the theatre the man beside him refused to stand or remove his hat for the national anthem. Gillespie found this too provoking. He picked a fight during which he broke his opponent's nose. A warrant was taken out against him for assault. Gillespie's small stature now came in useful. He escaped on board ship dressed as a woman, complete with borrowed baby in his arms. But it had been a close shave.

Pigeon's eye view of Comber's warrior hero. Note the sword wrongly positioned in his right hand.

Trouble and Gillespie went hand in hand. One night in San Domingo, when Gillespie was recovering from malaria, he heard a scream. Hastily snatching up his sword, he rushed downstairs and found the body of his faithful servant lying in a pool of blood. Behind it were a band of thieves brandishing weapons. Immediately the gang went for the comical-looking little man awaiting them in night attire on the stairs. Gillespie killed six before one of the intruders shot him, leaving him severely wounded. It was a good job that help was near at hand, and he soon recovered.

When his regiment returned to England in 1802, Lieutenant-Colonel Gillespie was absolutely adored by his men. But he found life at home quiet, and in 1805 applied for a transfer to India. Here occurred the famous ride from Arcot to Vellore, celebrated in a poem by Sir Henry Newbolt. Gillespie was out for a canter on his horse Black Bob, when a wounded man who had escaped from Vellore told him of the massacre of the British garrison there:

> Riding at dawn, riding alone,
> Gillespie left the town behind;
> Before he turned by the Westward road
> A horseman crossed him, staggering blind.

Losing no time, Gillespie led his troops to Vellore, where he blew open the gates of the fort and exacted a terrible revenge on the native princes, who had perpetrated the atrocity.

Gillespie had many adventures, both in India and on the island of Java. The names of his major battles are recorded on the memorial in Comber Square. By 1814 he had climbed to the rank of Major-General, and it was in that year that he met his end outside the fortress of Kalunga in Nepal. His last words, according to the monument, were, 'One shot more for the honour of Down', but there is dispute about this. Colleagues brought Gillespie's body, preserved in a barrel of rum, to Meerut where he is buried. His knighthood was posthumous, coming in the 1815 New Year's Honours List.

The Comber memorial was unveiled on 24th June 1845. It is a masonic monument, and on that day some fifty masonic lodges poured into Comber. It has been calculated that thirty thousand people witnessed the ceremony, which was reported in the *Illustrated London News*. A distant relative had posed for the statue. But why is Gillespie's sword in his right hand? (Gillespie was left-handed). And why is the date of his death wrongly recorded as 24th October? 31st October is correct. If you ever visit St. Paul's Cathedral in London, you will see another statue of Gillespie, an excellent sculpture in marble by Sir Francis Chantrey. On this statue the sword is correctly positioned in the left hand.

Finally, it is worth recording that another Gillespie is also commemorated on the Comber monument. This was our hero's grandson, also a Major-General called Robert Rollo, who fought in the Bengal army in India, and died in 1890.

6 Money, whiskey, linen and sweat

In the 1830s Comber was a small but busy industrial town, lying at the heart of a thriving agricultural district. Large amounts of flax were grown, and spinning was the chief occupation of the people. One of the finest hand spinners in the country was an extraordinary Comber lady called Anne McQuillan, a small, lively woman whose health and sight were alas ruined through her dedication to her art. Anne's speciality was superfine yarn. In one instance she spun a thread reputedly measuring 214 English miles in length, using a wheel made before the marriage of her grandmother in 1716! She regularly spun for Lady Dufferin who had her thread made into fine lace in London.

By the 1830s, however, hand spinning was in decline. Spinning was becoming mechanised, and being controlled by men like John Stitt, who had a spinning mill behind his fine house in the Square. In 1808-09 Stitt received £522 from the Linen Trustees for installing 348 spindles. The Stitts had their years in the sun, however by 1840 the family had become insolvent. One of the Andrews family, Isaac, snapped up their home, which became known as the 'big house', latterly best known as the car showrooms of Kane of Comber.

The Andrews family were by now Comber's 'merchant princes', by far the biggest players and employers in the emergent industrial town. John the Great had died in 1808, aged eighty-seven, and the family business was now headed by James, under the name of James Andrews and Sons. In 1812 his two elder boys became partners. John confined himself to buying and selling linen and farming, but William Glenny Andrews became master of every

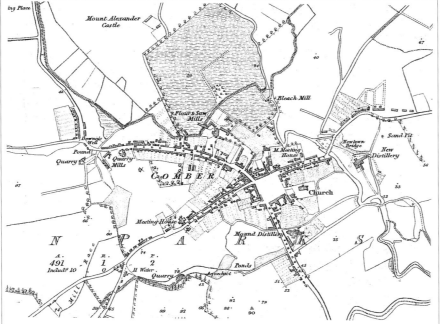

The 1834 Ordnance Survey map of Comber. Gillespie has not yet risen to his sentry post above the Square, and neither Second Comber nor the Unitarian churches yet exist. The building marked 'Church' is the earlier St. Mary's of the Scots settlers. The distilleries and flour mill represent Comber's industrial growth, but the railway has not yet come to the town and John Andrews spinning mill is still thirty years in the future. Note the large gardens – or rather vegetable patches!

section of the business. Later Thomas and Isaac also joined the firm. Four other sons entered the legal profession.

The 1830s saw major re-organisation and modernisation of the Andrews' 'empire'. A steam engine pumped water to either the flour mill or bleach works as occasion demanded. In addition, four new water wheels were erected, each powering different sections of the works. There was also a wheel at Castlebeg for the beetling engine, and another at the corn mill. The spring dam was completed in 1837 beside the bleach works. It was described as:

a pool of beautiful, pure soft water, superior, we think, to any we have seen, which will be of infinite value in finishing the nicer articles.

As well as being a producer of high quality linen goods, Comber was also a producer of paper. John Ward had a paper mill on the Newtownards Road until 1825,[1] when William Byrne took it over and converted it into a

Isaac Andrews (1799-1883), looking very much at peace with himself.

distillery. The Airsteps factory now occupies the site. A run-off from the Inler entered a dam behind the present Strickland's petrol station, then flowed alongside the distillery before re-entering the river. The distillery was thus isolated on an island, and was sometimes called the Island Distillery, although its more common name was the Lower Distillery. In 1834 its rateable value was the grand sum of twenty-nine pounds. All transactions were not above board, however, and in 1845 we are told that the excise collector reported the distiller for illegal removal of spirits.

The excise man didn't always win. The occasional bottle is said to have been thrown out the window, to float away into welcoming arms somewhere along the Inler. The owner of the welcoming arms would soon themselves be floating away into oblivion. One employee knocked a hole in the wall and ran a piece of hosepipe out through it. The elixir of life flowed out to his friend in the street. Soon word got around of a magical stone spouting out something that tasted suspiciously like whiskey, and before long half the population of Comber were running down the streets, wielding tin baths, saucepans and chamber pots, all intent on savouring this phenomenon. The following day, the strange disappearance of around a hundred gallons of whiskey was noticed. By then it was too late to do much about it, because most of the evidence had gone. The local constabulary, try as they might, could not get anyone to say anything about the disappearance.

A second distillery, the Upper Distillery, was also opened in 1825 by two local entrepreneurs, George Johnston and John Miller, in what had been a brewery in Barry Street (now Killinchy Street). Distilling was not new on this site. James Patterson, who died in 1763, had once owned a malt kiln and distillery here, and another former owner, William Murdock, is described on his tombstone in St. Mary's graveyard as 'the eminent distiller of Comber'.

The Upper Distillery was also known as 'The Mound Distillery' as there was a mound of earth between it and the Inler. Beside it was Waterford Loney or Lane, which forded the river. In later years this became Potale (pronounced pot-yal) Loney and is now Park Way. Potale was the remnants of the barley after the whiskey had been made. Farmers came with their box-carts to carry it away as cattle feed. The venture was a great initial success. In 1829-30 the Upper Distillery produced some eighty thousand gallons of whiskey, leading, no doubt, to much sagacious reflecting on life,

The Lower Distillery on the Newtownards Road, converted from a paper mill in 1825. All trace of this enterprise has now gone. The stream in the foreground is not the Inler, but a run-off from the river, which supplied the dam that stood where Strickland's petrol station now stands.

and equally, to many a hangover!

Though a certain amount of this barley was grown locally, Comber was chiefly corn and flax country. Its farmers were prosperous and progressive. The Ordnance Survey memoir describes them as respectable men, whose farm buildings were good and commodious. All let their land from the Londonderrys at a rent of between one and two guineas an acre, land nearest the town commanding a premium. Smaller landlords, who sublet, generally charged more.

According to the 1831 census, Comber parish had 558 agricultural labourers, most of whom were in regular work, at about a shilling per day. Women were employed during the harvest, while children helped with the planting and gathering of potatoes.

Labourers typically rented their cottages from farmers at about two pounds per annum, paid half-yearly. Ground for planting potatoes was generally rent-free. John Andrews (1792-1864), the agent for Lord Londonderry, described these farmers, who could be very penny conscious, as the 'most grinding landlords on earth'. Andrews was popular with the tenants. He was

John Andrews (1792-1864), agent for Lord Londonderry and founder of the flax spinning mill on the Ballygowan Road. John was liked by the tenants, who presented a magnificent illuminated address to his widow when he died.

a fair, liberal man, with a well-developed social conscience, qualities that his master, the third Lord Londonderry, rather lacked. In 1826 he married Sarah Drennan, daughter of Dr. William Drennan, one of the founders of the United Irishmen, and the poet who coined the phrase 'the emerald isle'. Andrews' attributes were officially recognised in 1857, when he was appointed High Sheriff of County Down.

The Andrews family farmed several hundred acres in the 1830s, taking a great general interest in farming. John's father, James, was a founder member of the North East Society, forerunner of the Royal Ulster Agricultural Society, and his livestock regularly won prizes. James' sons shared his interest in agricultural improvement. John's pamphlet on scientific farming was distributed to the tenants, while William Glenny Andrews published a paper on the treatment of flax. Peter Bernard in his *Tour of Inspection through Ulster* in 1823 says:

In no part of Ireland or the Netherlands that I have visited, have I seen flax in the field of so good a quality as that grown in the immediate neighbourhood of Comber.

You might have expected a town such as Comber to have a market, but none existed in the 1830s. This would soon be rectified, however, and in 1841 we read of the town's new market house. Big quarterly fairs were held on 5th January, 5th April, 28th June and 19th October. These fairs were tremendous occasions, attracting farmers, traders, entertainers, hucksters and ne'er do wells from across the county and beyond. For the most part of the century these fairs, alongside potatoes and whiskey, were Comber's greatest claim to fame.

In 1837 the town's growing population was served by ten grocers, twenty masons, twenty carpenters, six smiths, fifteen shoemakers, ten tailors and three ironmongers. There were also nineteen public houses, to which John McCance, the town's Presbyterian minister, attributed 'almost all the wickedness and misery that surround us'. But it seems that Comber was quiet and peaceable. There were generally no more than two policemen in the barracks in Newtown Street, and they had little to do. A manor court for cases of debt and dispute was held on the third Thursday of the month in Barry's inn by Alexander Montgomery, the attorney.

The patronage of the Londonderrys was beneficial to the town. In 1813 a parochial (i.e. Church of Ireland) school had been set up in Comber Square, built jointly by the wife of the second marquess and the Erasmus Smyth

Class of 1910, Londonderry school, Comber Square. Opened in 1813, the school remained operational until the big amalgamation of 1938.

Charity. This was a single storey building with two rooms and a small playground in front. In 1837 it had 233 pupils – 137 boys and 96 girls, mostly protestant but including eight Roman Catholics. School attendance was not compulsory. The master received thirty pounds yearly from the Charity, and one halfpenny weekly from each of the pupils who were able to pay. In 1832 a house was built for the master behind the school. The school continued until 1938. In 1954 it was demolished and replaced by St. Mary's parochial hall.

By 1837 there were two other schools in Comber. That in Hill Street (now High Street) was established in 1831 by the Hibernian Society. It was held in what are now the lower committee and minister's rooms of First Comber Presbyterian Church, and had sixty-six protestant pupils. A private school in Barry Street, established in 1827, had thirty-five protestant pupils. A fourth school had by this time closed due to 'the indisposition of the master'.

The town expanded along the four main streets which radiated from the central square. In 1837 there were 355 houses in the town, of which 184 were one-storied. Most were slated, although thirty-five were thatched. The town was not considered particularly attractive. Some mud cabins, of varying quality, remained, but most of the dwellings were built of local greywacke,

*Charles, third Lord Londonderry (1778–
1854), owner of the town.*

which gave them a 'stark and heavy appearance'. However, things were
looking up. The newer houses were being built in Scrabo sandstone, which
was thought to be a great improvement.

There was poverty too. According to the 1831 census, twenty-four houses
in the town were inhabited by more than one family. Bedding was described
as 'frequently poor and scanty'. When the third Lord Londonderry inspected
the town in 1841 he had some scathing comments to make. He found that
'the sewers in all the streets are little attended to', special mention being
made of houses next to the meeting house that 'require attention to carry
their dunghills and sewers to their rears'. In those days, most houses had no
back doors, with the result that slops, filth and rubbish were pitched out on
to the street. No wonder diseases such as tuberculosis were rife. In addition,
the school was 'neglected', a neglect Lord Londonderry attributed to 'sloth'.
Londonderry wanted the inn yard kept clean, and a nasty outbuilding
belonging to Mr. Stitt made less unsightly. St. Mary's needed 'decent rough-
cast or whitewashing' on the glebe house side. And he fires a salvo at the
glebe house waterspouts, which he found 'perfectly unaccountable and

views who had never subscribed to the Westminster Confession of Faith. On his departure, several members of the congregation, influenced by his preaching, broke away to form a separate Unitarian congregation in the town. John Miller, who owned the distillery, made a room available in his home for Unitarian meetings. Later a loft was fitted out for Sunday evening lectures, given by a number of liberal clergymen. These meetings attracted some of the leading figures in the town, including James Andrews, who officiated as elder.[2]

As Unitarian numbers grew, John Miller hoped to build a church on high ground opposite his office at the Upper Distillery in Killinchy Street. With John Andrews' help, a lease was agreed on the land. However, certain persons objected, arguing that the people to whom the lease was being given were members of the Liberal Party, and that it would not be right to grant it. And so John Miller did not get the lease. This went to another breakaway group who were to become Second Comber Presbyterian Church. They must have been largely Tory!

But it was not over yet. James Andrews had intended to build a new house on Windmill Hill. He now generously gave this site to the Unitarian Church for a new meeting house. William Hugh Doherty became its first

John Miller, Unitarian benefactor. Described as having the 'look of a porpoise without flippers', Miller was in fact a very successful businessman, who put Old Comber Whiskey on the map.

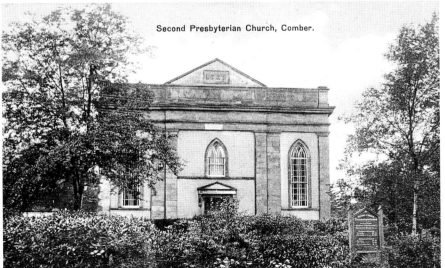

Second Presbyterian Church, Comber.

Second Comber Presbyterian Church in 1927, the year Rev. James E. Jones began his forty-two year ministry. How well it looks amidst all its greenery, now vanished.

minister in 1838. He remained in Comber until 1850 when he emigrated to America. But the opening of the new church was held up for over a year by the momentous storm that took place on the night of January 6th-7th 1839, the legendary 'night of the big wind'. Awesome damage was caused on that fearful night. The distillery in Killinchy Street was blown down, as was the huge chimney of Andrews' flour mill. The damage to the church was caused when the top of the windmill blew off and landed on the roof. The congregation somehow emerged triumphantly from these adverse beginnings.

Meanwhile, Isaac Nelson had become the new minister at the original Presbyterian meeting house. However, a number of members of his new congregation were not happy, and they tried to get rid of him. The conservative theologian, Dr. Henry Cooke, intervened, suggesting that the best course might be to establish a second congregation in the town. Apart from the difference of opinion over Nelson, more church accommodation was needed. And so in 1838 the new congregation of Second Comber assembled for worship in a loft near the bottom of High Street, in what later became Milling's yard.

This new congregation of about seventy families chose the Rev. John Rogers as their minister. He was ordained in 1839. Lord Londonderry granted ground to the congregation at a nominal rent, and the new meeting house in Killinchy Street opened for worship in 1840. The congregation grew and, in the year of revival of 1859, an increase in numbers is recorded due to the wave of religious fervour. John Rogers remained as minister until 1869, achieving the distinction of being elected Moderator of the General Assembly in 1863 and 1864.

7 Railway town

Steam trains aren't everyone's cup of tea. They're noisy, dirty, awkward looking beasts – and you have to travel a bit to meet one these days if you live in Comber. But that wasn't always the case. For Comber was once at the very heart of the BCDR, or 'The oul County Down' as it was known. The main line from Belfast came through here on its way to Newcastle, and another line branched off to Newtownards and Donaghadee. So Comber station was an important junction. The first trains ran on 6th May 1850, carrying about one thousand passengers on that day. In those early days there were five trains a day, taking around twenty-five minutes to reach Comber from Belfast. You would have sat in a flat-sided four-wheeled

The Harland and Wolff diesel electric locomotive approaches Comber station from Ballygowan. The junction to Newtownards can be seen veering off to the left along what is now the by-pass.

Comber station. Here we can contrast the old and the new – a horse and cart alongside a new fangled motor car.

carriage with oil lighting, and the locomotive would have been very basic, with no weather protection for the driver or fireman.

The line reached Donaghadee in 1861 and Newcastle in 1869. By 1893 the section from Belfast to Comber was doubled due to the volume of traffic, while at 832 feet (254 metres) Comber's platforms were the longest on the whole BCDR system. Guy Stone of Comber (1808-62), who lived at Barnhill on the Belfast Road, was for a time chairman of the BCDR, and later on Thomas Andrews of Ardara held the same position. Barnhill is still known as Stones' Plantin'. The Stone family had early and abiding links with the Orange Order, and the first parade in the district was held in one of their fields in the late 1790s.

The entrance to the station was off the Glen Road. However, during the 1920s steps were constructed, giving access to the street beside the North Down House. Two subways went under the track, with glass square-sets at strategic points providing some light in daylight hours. The three waiting rooms always revealed a cheery coal fire on a cold winter's night. Vending machines displayed their wares, but not everyone used money in exchange for their bar of chocolate. Washers the size of an old penny would do the trick just as well! Eason's newspaper kiosk was open at peak hours, ably managed for many years by Madge Watson. This business was eventually purchased by Gordon Smyth whose shop was in Comber Square. Later still, James Miskelly ran it from his home in Castle Street. Incidentally, it was James Miskelly who first sold sticks of rock with the word Comber in them.

James Miskelly in his shop in Castle Street in the 1950s, surrounded by jars of sweets, bars of chocolate, and bottles of 'pop'.

Farmers knew the 'dinner train', the 'milking train' and the 'quitin' train'. If anyone took out their watch, it was to set it by the train! Bicycles were a common sight in the station. Alex Neil recalled:

The shipyard men rode their bikes up to the station to get the early morning train. The bikes were still going when they leapt into the train as it was starting to leave. There was wheels, pedals and handlebars everywhere, and my job each day was to put them into some sort of order to stop other passengers from falling over them!

Comber originally had two signal boxes, the North Box above Middleton's garage and the South box at the junction of the main and branch lines. Both became redundant in 1926 with the building of a central cabin on the station platform. One signalman called Willie McConnell was known to knit scarves and jumpers. Various members of the Johnston family were stationmasters. David John Johnston received two awards for bravery on the railway. One of these related to an incident at Comber, when a Mr. Kelly from Ringneil fell off the platform in front of a train. Johnston leapt forward and at great danger to himself threw Mr. Kelly clear at the last moment. Many travellers witnessed this event, and were loud in their praise for the rescuer.

Staff at Comber station around 1920. Seated (l-r) Alex Neill (ticket clerk), George Swindle (signalman), William Johnston (stationmaster). Standing – Andy McGowan (porter), George Dunbar (head porter), Sam Thompson (boy porter).

As well as passenger traffic Comber saw the movement of a great diversity of goods – farm produce and livestock, whiskey, coal, flax and yarn, grain, quarry stone, building materials, fish, and all the other freight that railways usually carried. Horses and carts were a familiar sight on their way to and from the goods yard. Tom Corken Senior recalled the hard graft involved when shovelling coal from the wagons into the carts. 'Two of us would have shovelled all day and cleared two ten-ton wagons. I was young and fit then!'

After leaving Comber station, the railway crossed the Glen Road bridge, before going alongside Railway Street, where a siding curved into the Andrews spinning mill. Some half mile past the Ballygowan Road level crossing, the main line disappeared into a deep narrow cutting known as 'the gullet'. The gradient was steep, and heavy goods trains sometimes ground to a halt here. It was too much for the huge, eighty-two ton 'Baltic Tanks'. George Dunbar remembers:

One of them was hauling a goods train and the couplings broke about a mile out as she was coming into Comber from Ballygowan. Some of the wagons were left behind unknown to the engine men. They only realised what had happened when they stopped at Comber, and by then it was too late. The stray wagons came down the gradient by themselves and bashed into the back of the train. It took the railway all day to clear up the wreckage.

The Baltics never worked the main line again.

The Donaghadee branch curved left after leaving the station, crossing the spinning mill dam. There was a small pump-house here where engines could replenish their tanks. The line then went under High Street before crossing Killinchy Street. The gatekeeper here in the 1920s was Grace Hiles, whose five-year old son John was killed by a train in 1926. Tragedy struck again when Tommy Cairns was killed at the same spot in 1943 in heavy snow. It appears that the snow had muffled the sound of the oncoming train.

The 'Glassmoss' crossing was on the Newtownards Road. However, the actual Glassmoss – where glass-making sand used to be dug – was further along at the Island Hill Road. When the Ards Tourist Trophy (TT) motor race was run from 1928-36, temporary platforms were built on each side of the road, with a wooden footbridge connecting them. Passengers simply walked over the bridge and changed trains. Clever stuff! The very railway lines – said to be the only section of BCDR rail surviving in its original track bed – can still be seen in the road at the next crossing on the Ballyhenry Road.

The excursion trains on their way to the seaside were a fine sight. On a Saturday you could have watched the 'Golfer's Express' pass on its way to Newcastle. And from 1933 you might have seen the diesel-electric locomotive

Train at Comber station.

One of Sammy Davidson's buses at the opening of Ardmillan Orange Hall in 1924. The photo shows his driver, Robert Gibson.

built by Harland and Wolff. This was the first locomotive of its type in the world. Other trains included cattle and horse-box specials, Twelfth of July demonstration trains and, of course, excursions to the TT race. As many as 27,000 passengers were carried to Comber on a race day.

The main line to Newcastle closed in January 1950. April 22nd 1950 saw the very last train from Comber station, and on that day an impressive number turned out to bid farewell to the railway era. Some railway staff were absorbed into the road services. But what a let down! George Dunbar, a signalman with a lifetime of knowledge and expertise, received his letter of transfer. And what was his new job? Bus cleaner at a Belfast depot!

Closure had been on the cards for some time. Cars and buses provided routes right into town centres and past the front doors of people's houses. As early as the 1920s Sammy Davidson, who had a grocery shop and coal yard at the bottom of Killinchy Street, was running a service to Belfast in his buses called 'Iona' and 'Myona'. And Tommy Crosby had a taxi. His garage was under the Thompson Hall in Mill Street. Road freight services were also appearing. Railway revenues declined.

In January 1945 a horrific accident at Ballymacarrett brought the sort of publicity that the weakened railway could ill afford. Then in 1948 the Ulster Transport Authority took over. In Comber station you would have seen a change of uniform and tickets. Some of the locomotives were now painted black instead of the BCDR dark green. But just a few months later, it was decided to close down most of Northern Ireland's railway network, including the line to Comber. A protest meeting was held in Andrews Memorial Hall in 1949, but to no avail.

For a time Comber station was used as a ticket office and store for the buses. Many of us can still remember the UTA double and single deckers in their green and white livery. The tracks lay for some three years before being lifted. One by one the buildings came down – the water tower at Laureldale, the weighbridge at Railway Street, the signal boxes, the cattle beach and crane in the goods yard. Someone made off with the lead guttering from the station's roof. Finally in 1962 a new by-pass was unfurled along the track bed. All that remains today of Comber's grand railway heritage is the old goods shed, retained for many years as a council store and tastefully converted to a fire station in 1996. C'est la vie.

8 Molly's world

Some years ago a datestone marked 1867 was found in a stone wall in the car park at the rear of Supervalu. It marked the site of a garden that once ran from the Old House, home of the Andrews family, to the river. We have already met 'honest' John Andrews, the agent of Lord Londonderry. His niece, Molly Drennan, spent a large part of her childhood here, and she has left us an intriguing account of her life in Comber during the period from 1860-76. The Old House already had a lengthy history in Molly's day. Here is her very un-misty-eyed description of it:

The house where we were so happy was a very ugly three-storied one in the village street, facing north, and inconvenient in many ways. It had been added to and altered, but in an unattractive way. The third storey where the nurseries had been was reached by a steep stair like a ladder; an addition had been made by breaking a door through to a small house next door (I never saw such a house with so many doors) and the sitting rooms looked out directly on the street, while the bedrooms, many of them, were little cubby holes.

The extensive gardens of the house covered what are now the tennis courts, and much of the present car park. Unfortunately, to reach them you had to cross a yard where an old turkey cock gobbled about among the hens and geese. Molly was quite terrified of this horrible creature, and when going out took care to sneak round it. Then a broad avenue led through the flowerbeds to the centre of the garden, while down by the river were rhododendrons and a sumach tree. Beside these was a circular pond, which

Molly's 'place', as seen from the air in 1929. The Old House (bottom right, opposite Uraghamore, extreme right) was demolished in 1956. The big gardens are now a car park and tennis courts.

has now been built over. In Molly's day it was full of weeds, lilies, sticklebacks, and tiny frogs. People are known to have drowned in this pond.

Molly describes the little nooks and workshops in and around her play area – 'the place', as she called it. She recalls the stables and coach houses, where Jacob Gibson sat mending the harness. At Henry Morrison, the smith's, you could quench your thirst from a rusty tin mug and admire his dahlia planted in a big iron pot in the middle of a little stream. Behind William Lindsey the carpenter's shop was a row of pigsties facing the river. And you could be weighed in the mill scales by George Jervis, the big miller.

Molly vividly remembers the Andrews family of her day. John Andrews actually lived at Uraghamore, and Molly's memories are of a kind, silent old gentleman of whom she was in awe. He always seemed to be pruning the peach trees and winding the clocks. His wife Sarah ('auntmama') was a small, wrinkled lady with blue eyes and auburn hair. After John's death she always wore black. The Old House itself was occupied by William Glenny Andrews, who never married, and his sisters Margaret and Mary. William Glenny was a fine old gentleman with very white hair and shabby old-fashioned clothes. He was kind, but could at times be seen in a dreadful passion, shaking his fist at men in the yard. Margaret was crippled with rheumatism, while Mary is remembered for doling out gingerbread cakes and grapes.

We also have Molly's descriptions of John's three sons. James had projecting, short-sighted eyes and his mother's curly hair. He was fond of literature and a bit of a philosopher. Johnnie was the prankster of the family, chasing the children round tables and grabbing at their ankles. He was a keen sportsman, with a love of horses and dogs. Tommy (of Ardara) was tall, plodding and persevering. But Molly's greatest friend and companion was John's daughter Fanny, who made little wreaths of holly, and decorated the house at Christmas. Molly worshipped her.

Molly wrote her reminiscences in 1915. When she returned to Comber in 1947 she was saddened by what she found:

The Square House empty and blinded with creepers. The Old House neglected and a cinema next door. Uraghamore turned into two shops. The front garden a grassy desert… I shall see them always as they were. The present is no matter. I had happy days there. They cannot change.

Molly no doubt would be even more distressed if she could return today. For the Old House is no more. First it became a cinema, then a supermarket. One last remaining tree, an evergreen Irish oak, stood in Castle Street – until 1979 that is! Then it was cut down, causing much consternation.

Though they were Comber's biggest magnates, the Andrews family did not sit on their laurels. They remained as entrepreneurial as ever. Storage of

William Glenny Andrews (1793-1871).

There was an outcry when this old oak tree, the last belonging to the Old House, was felled in 1979. Here the ladders are up. The demolition work has begun.

grain in Belfast was becoming very expensive. So in 1859 Molly's uncle, William Glenny Andrews, commissioned a huge, six-storied grain store in Comber, erected close to the present leisure centre. It was completed in December 1863, having been built by local labour at a cost of £1,750. Over the years this imposing structure had many uses. The distillery stored barley in it, and before the First World War it was used by a Dutchman named Stem for the manufacture of rice starch. It is sometimes referred to as the 'old starch mill'.

During the Second World War American troops were billeted in the building. After the war it was used by two retired Indian Army colonels as a piggery. One of the colonels was the father of Paddy Ashdown, former leader of the Liberal Democrat Party, and it was in Comber that Paddy spent his boyhood days. One summer evening in July 1978 vandals set fire to the grain store. Though the fire services fought hard, pouring over one hundred thousand gallons of water on the building, it was totally gutted and had to be bulldozed to the ground. Molly would have been horrified.

In 1863 Molly's uncle, John Andrews, embarked on an even more ambitious venture, a linen spinning mill on the Ballygowan Road. His son Thomas, then only twenty years old, superintended the building operations. Spinning commenced in June 1864, but John did not survive to see the opening of his mill. He had passed away just a few weeks previously. An illuminated address was presented to the Andrews family by the tenants of Lord Londonderry on the occasion of his death. The paintings in it portray Comber as Molly would have known it. Many of the Andrews family are buried in the family vault in St. Mary's churchyard, erected by William Glenny Andrews in 1867. But although there are large bays inside for holding coffins, for legal reasons all burials are in a further vault below ground.

When the first week's wages were paid to the spinning mill workers, a machine boy received five pence per week, a doffer four pence, and a spinning master four shillings and twopence. A doffer was the person who removed the full bobbins of yarn from the machines. The spinning master was expected to set an example. When Robert Forsythe applied for the position in 1871 he was brusquely warned that 'unless you are strictly sober you need not think of coming to us'. Some of the staff gained reputations as outstanding workers, for instance Grace Ritchie, who was described as a 'doffing mistress and

Grain store, rice starch mill, piggery – this massive six-storied building had many names and uses. Remarkable for its scale if not its beauty, it was gutted by a fire started by vandals in 1978.

first class worker' when she left the company to emigrate to America.

Although the Andrews family tried to create a safe working environment, accidents did happen. In a letter to Dr James Frame in 1865 it was stated that:

Yesterday a doffer in the mill lost a finger in the fencing of a spinning frame which was properly fenced. By her own neglect and through forgetfulness she allowed her hand to get too close to the fencing.

Unfortunately the tendency was to blame the poor victim. Four years later Eliza Gabbey had her hand amputated after it caught in the draft gearing of a spinning frame.

The Andrews' were paternalistic employers. The mill had its own school in Mill View, once called Duck Hole View because there was a pond with ducks there. An evening school operated from 1867-78 for mill workers who wished to improve their education. In 1877 a day school opened to teach employees' children.

After the death of John Andrews, the company was for a time rudderless. And rudderless in the face of adversity. The bleach works closed in 1872, and from 1868-76 there was a steady loss of some two thousand pounds a

The Andrews' flax spinning mill, 1864. This huge structure, which looks like it belongs in a big industrial city, not a small country town, shows the scale of Andrews' ambition. Note the train in the right foreground.

year. Then Isaac's son, John, returned to Comber and was given sole control. By 1877 the business was back in profit. But Comber would not be the beneficiary. In 1883 John and his brother decided to transfer the flour milling business to Belfast under the name of Isaac Andrews & Sons, and the Comber flour mill closed, although the office remained in use until 1885. In 1882 an experimental telephone line was installed from here to the new mill in Belfast, said to be the first taken out into the country. The redundant flour mill was eventually demolished around 1900. The stones from it were used to build McBurney's Row in Castle Lane. The spinning mill continued under Thomas Andrews of Ardara, and was enlarged in 1907. Around 1900 Thomas also demolished the Upper Corn Mill, where the Andrews' entrepreneurial adventure had begun.

The Andrews' did not of course have a complete monopoly of industry in Comber. John Miller (1796-1883), the Unitarian, was another significant local industrialist.[1] By 1860 he had taken over both distilleries, and was

Mill workers take a break from their labours. Note the drive belts along the ceiling, which powered the machines.

operating them as a single enterprise, producing the famous 'Old Comber' whiskey. Like the other members of Comber's merchant aristocracy, he lived in the heart of the town. Molly recalls attending country dances at his home, 'Aureen' in the Square. She described him as a very fat man with short arms, 'which gave him the look of a porpoise with flippers'. The name 'Miller' can be seen today on the edge of the footpath in front of 'Aureen', picked out in white cobblestones. Also depicted is a hare, along with what is said to be the champion greyhound Master McGra and his trainer. Master McGra was owned by Lord Lurgan, whose family name (Brownlow) is perpetuated in Brownlow Street. A less romantic, but probably correct, explanation of this intriguing piece of street art is that it depicts nothing more than an ordinary hunting scene.

Around 1873 Miller sold both distilleries to Samuel Bruce, who lived in Gloucestershire and installed a resident partner called McCance. The firm had around sixty employees and an output in 1887 of some 150,000 gallons of pot-still whiskey from each distillery, which is a lot of juice. Five excise officers were employed in that year, the chief being Thomas Galway. These men ensured that the distilleries paid the correct amount of excise duty on the whiskey they produced. Comber whiskies were matured for up to twenty

OLD
COMBER WHISKEY

GUARANTEED   10 YEARS OLD
PURE   POT STILL

OLD
COMBER
WHISKEY

BOTTLED   IN BOND
AT THE   DISTILLERIES

COMBER

FAC-SIMILE OF BOTTLE AND LABEL

Comber Distilleries Co. Ltd.,
COMBER,
Co Down, Ireland.

Old Comber Whiskey. The odd bottle can still be found – at a price! Despite occasional rumours that the Old Comber brand might be re-launched, it is unlikely that distilling would take place here.

years and had an excellent reputation. In 1894, for instance, Lord Londonderry gave a glass or two of the precious nectar to the Prince of Wales, later King Edward VII, who enjoyed it so much that Lord Londonderry later presented him with several gallons of the stuff.

Molly's playground lay close to the Ralph brothers' tannery. Horner's pharmacy today occupies the site. The story goes that when the inspector came to grade and stamp the hides of leather, one of the brothers would take him across to Milling's Hotel for refreshment, while the other brother proceeded to stamp the hides that were below standard. On his return, the inspector was probably oblivious to the difference. A row of houses in Castle Lane was known locally as Tanner's Row because most of the occupants worked at the tannery.

James George Allen was another of the Square's more prominent residents. He was a clever engineer who in his spare time built a motor car, the first to be seen in the Comber district. He also took over Ralph's tan-yard, where he constructed traction engines and steamrollers. You can still see traces of furnaces in the wall as you walk along the path beside Horner's shop to the car park.[2] Allen tested his engines around the town. One frosty morning he had a nasty accident at the railway crossing on the Newtownards Road. His engine skidded, crashing into a bread cart and killing the two horses that pulled it.

Castle Espie. The former industrial complex is now a wildfowl sanctuary.

Moving a little outside Molly's immediate environment, we come to the Castle Espie industrial complex, about two and a half miles outside Comber on the Ballydrain Road. There had been a limestone works here from at least the 1630s, the lime being used by farmers to enrich their land. Then in 1864 Robert Murland developed the lime quarries, installing twenty-four German Hoffman kilns, capable of producing six hundred tons of burnt lime per week. The Hoffmans also served to fire the upper layer of clay, which was to be used for making bricks. Many thousands of bricks were produced, and they can be found in some of Comber's older buildings. All bore the name Castle Espie on one side. Murland also constructed a massive sea wall and a pier, which carried a narrow gauge railway. The 173 foot (53 metre) high chimney of the boiler house was the second tallest in Ireland. Glazed pottery was also produced here for a short time. The works closed for good in 1878, and the chimney was demolished in 1912.

Today Castle Espie is home to the Wildfowl and Wetlands Centre, a sanctuary for the wildlife of Strangford Lough. Strangford is particularly renowned for teal, widgeon, oystercatchers and Brent geese. Some of these migrate from as far away as Canada.[3] The former limestone and clay pits have been converted into a series of ponds, now given over to wild life.

As we have seen, manufacturing and farming were the twin props of the local economy. This was prospering, as witnessed by the opening of a bank in 1850 and the erection of a market house in the 1840s, behind the present police station in Killinchy Street (then Market Street). There was a market here every Tuesday for potatoes, hay, straw and turnips. But Bassett, in his 1886 Directory, tells us that, in spite of the organiser's best efforts, the market floundered owing to the nearness of Belfast. The market house was taken over by the distillery after World War One, and finally knocked down in the 1950s.

The market house was used for more than trade. Around 1850 an infant school was held upstairs, and at some stage Father Close began to celebrate mass there every Sunday. 1863 finds the town's Roman Catholics worshipping in a building in the Crescent, later a blacksmith's shop. The Roman Catholic Church of the Visitation of the Blessed Virgin in Killinchy Street opened for worship in 1872. It is in the Early Gothic style and built of Scrabo stone. A school was built at the beginning of the twentieth century,

Comber market house seen in mid-picture with a horse and cart outside the entrance. The house with the ornate chimneys (bottom right) was originally the distillery manager's residence.

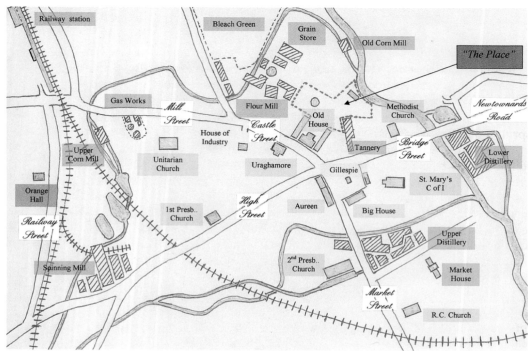

Comber in Molly's day.

and when it became too small, the present school was opened in 1955.

Molly will also have known another, much less august 'market house', an old wooden hut which for many years sat under the shadow of Gillespie in the Square. This 'market house', as it was derisively known, was owned by the distillery, and beside it was a weighbridge where the farmers brought their barley on a Thursday. What did Molly think of it? An interesting snippet appears in the *Newtownards Chronicle* in 1874, allegedly written by Comber's most famous citizen, Sir Robert Rollo himself, who has recently had a clean-up and is none too pleased by the monstrosity beside him:

When I look down from my elevated position and see that most detestable shed, I am grieved and wonder how any party could ever think of putting it there to disgrace me, and insult the noble and generous parties who put me here… But if I could get down (as I cannot now, for the painters have taken away the ladders) I would get powder and send the whole edifice in true balloon style to the Glass Moss, where there is plenty of room, and few to see it but the goats.

But the offending structure stayed. In the 1920s the hut and weighbridge were taken over by James Milling, who ran a thriving business in the Square.[4] Milling sold groceries, wines and spirits and all sorts of merchandise, and in addition was a horse dealer and a funeral undertaker. Mr Milling also manufactured mineral waters, and it is said that he discovered his mineral spring as the result of a persistent dream.

The Comber churches remained active, playing their part not only in the religious life of the community, but also in the education of its children. The great revival of 1859 broke out in County Down when a group of converts from Ballymena arrived at First Comber. Soon afterwards the Rev. Killen was addressing a prayer meeting at which many people were reduced to tears on account of their sins, and some had to be removed after fainting. In Mr. Killen's words:

The whole town and neighbourhood were roused. Many did not retire to rest the first night at all, and for several days great numbers were unable to attend to their usual avocations, but gave themselves almost unceasingly to the study of the scriptures, singing and prayer... Altogether we have had above three hundred and fifty cases of visible awakening in our congregation... Drunkards have been reformed, prostitutes reclaimed, thieves have become honest... Our converts include children of seven and old men and women of upwards of seventy years of age.

The Rev. Killen's name can be found today on a rather weathered

Clergy commemorate the centenary of Comber's Catholic church in 1972. The Bishop of Down and Connor, the Most Rev. Dr. Philbin, is pictured centre right.

inscription on the outside wall of the Minor Hall of First Comber Presbyterian Church, 'erected 1869 Rev. J.M. Killen DD Pastor'. This was the building which became Comber National School, and in 1903 it had 208 pupils. The church itself got a complete face-lift in 1887 during the brief ministry of Robert Hanna. The roof, galleries, flooring and pews were all removed and the interior completely reconstructed. Two major alterations have taken place since. Firstly, in 1914 electric light and a splendid new organ were installed. Then in 1921, the present war memorial pulpit was erected.

'Down the hill' at Second Comber, a manse was built in 1860 at the rear of the meeting house. And in 1861 Second Comber got its own school, aided by a generous grant of seven hundred pounds from John Smyth of New Comber House. The school was thus called the Smyth National School. The building was extended in 1881, and demolished in 1993, to be replaced by a modern hall. By this time it had long ceased to be a schoolhouse.

Rev. John Orr was installed in the Unitarian Church in 1850. He also got a new manse, built in 1859. The minister's salary in 1865 was £150. It was of great benefit to have someone like John Miller in the congregation. In 1871 Millar had the church stone finished in Portland cement at his own expense. The burying ground was consecrated in 1863 and a church hall built in 1878, not long before Thomas Dunkerly became minister. From 1871 Fanny Andrews played the harmonium here. This was the cousin whom Molly adored, the girl for whom her neighbour, the carpenter William Lindsey had made a doll's house, back in those fondly remembered days when little Molly was a child.

9 A town mourns

The last two decades of the nineteenth and the first decade of the twentieth century was a period of stability rather than growth. The 'action' in these years was in the countryside, not the town. This period saw the biggest change in rural life in centuries, the transfer of ownership of the land from the great landlords to the humble people who farmed it.

In the 1880s, however, the farmers' main worry was rent. Many leases on the Londonderry estate had been set during the boom years of the 1850s. But things had since become very tough. Produce prices were falling. Labour costs had doubled. By the 1880s farming was in crisis. In 1888 the sixth Lord Londonderry responded by offering a twenty per cent reduction in rents, and surprised everyone by offering to sell his estate to the tenants if they paid the equivalent of their rents less twenty per cent for the next forty-nine years.[1]

Lord Londonderry wanted to sell his lands because he believed that owner-occupancy was the key to solving the Irish Question. By 1894 half his estate had been sold. By 1914 there were very few agricultural tenants left. The transfer of the land was almost complete.

The land question coloured local political attitudes. Somewhat surprisingly given modern allegiances, many local Presbyterian farmers were home rulers, feeling that their interests would be better represented in a Dublin, rather than a London parliament. However, with the disappearance of land grievances, Home Rule sentiment waned.

The prevailing sentiment became Unionist and Orange. As we have seen,

Folk art. This imposing Orange arch straddled High Street in the 1920s. The tradition of making arches has, alas, largely disappeared.

Orangeism in Comber dates back to the 1790s. The first local lodge seems to have been the Comber True Blues (LOL 1035), which may date back to 1819-23, although the present warrant dates from 1860, when they met in Paddy Ward's loft in Mill Street.[2] Comber Old Standard (LOL 567) followed in 1831, timing which suggests its founding had something to do with protestant fears over Catholic emancipation. This lodge had a long association with the Stone family of Barnhill, and its 1936 banner carried a painting of Bessie Stone.

Goldsprings of Comber (LOL 1037), known as the 'gouldies', got their first warrant in 1861 and met at John Young's in Bridge Street. Comber White Flag (LOL 244) was formed in 1875, and drew its original membership from the workers at Andrews Mill. This lodge has distinctive white collarettes. Some say they derive from a Temperance Movement called the Rachabites. Others link the colour white with purity, while still more point to its association with the mill and white linen. It is anybody's guess as to which is correct. Comber Ulster Defenders (LOL 100) was formed as an ex-serviceman's lodge in 1925. One side of their banner depicts an infantryman going over the top at the Somme. The other side shows three Comber soldiers – Bruce, De Wind and McRoberts.

The four seasonal fair days remained the liveliest and most important in the local calendar. Those held in April and October were hiring fairs where people offered themselves for sale. The town heaved as people, animals and hucksters of every shade and hue filed in from the surrounding countryside. Bargains were pursued, deals were clinched. There was drinking, haggling, promenading and much bustle. The *Newtownards Chronicle* reports on one such October fair:

…buyers were numerous, farmers looking for stock that could be turned to profitable account by feeding during the winter, while fleshers were on the look out for cattle… There were great numbers of farm servants looking for new places, and the prices at which they were engaged were higher than have been given at any former period… police…were drafted in from Newtownards and the districts adjoining Comber to preserve order, but their services were not called into active requisition, though, as usual, there was some disturbance and numbers of drunken people on the streets.

Sadly, the great fairs ceased around the time of the First World War. The markets also petered out. This marked the beginning of the town's commercial decline. Instead of buying locally, increasing numbers of shoppers travelled to Newtownards, especially on Saturdays. The agricultural workforce also started to decline. Paradoxically, this commercial 'winding down' took place against the backdrop of a rising population, a pattern that has unfortunately

Country town. Looking down Braeside towards the spinning mill, c.1900.

Thomas Andrews (1873-1912), the designer of the Titanic, *who went down with his ship, a hero to the last.*

been repeated in the last few years. Up until this time the population had remained relatively stable. In 1841 it stood at 1,964. In 1901 it was 2,095. However, by 1911 the population had risen to 2,686. This period also saw the beginning of commuting, as local people went to work in places like the ropeworks and the Belfast shipyards.

Further difficulties arose in 1898 when Comber was omitted from the progressive Town Improvement Act. Improvements which were obligatory elsewhere were not carried out here. However, there was some progress. The town got a new cemetery in 1894 – it might not live better, but it could now die better. The first person buried there was Martha McDowell of Troopersfield on the Ballygowan Road.[3] James Milling probably arranged the funeral. The town also acquired new public lighting, and a sewage system which 'thoroughly flushed three or four times a day automatically'.

For many years Comber remained the archetypal small Irish market town, a place where everybody knew everybody else and all the goings on. But one event stands out. It concerns a ship, and that ship was the mighty *Titanic*, which in 1912 went down off the coast of Newfoundland after hitting an iceberg on its maiden voyage. Around 1,500 perished in what was one of the

The great liner's dramatic last moments.

worst disasters in maritime history. But what has all this to do with Comber? The connection lies in Thomas Andrews.

Thomas Andrews was born in Comber in 1873, the second son of Thomas of Ardara and Eliza Pirrie. After leaving school he entered the shipyard, gaining an excellent knowledge of all aspects of shipbuilding. By 1905 he was head of the design department of Harland and Wolff, and in March 1907 he became managing director. He was involved in constructing many giant transatlantic liners for the White Star Line, including the *Olympic*, and its sister ship *Titanic*. Thomas not only designed the *Titanic*, he was also on the fateful voyage, and was one of those who didn't return. According to reports, he was a hero to the last, seen throwing chairs and other buoyant objects to people in the water right up to the end.

The Thomas Andrews Memorial Hall, a suitably sumptuous tribute.

When the news reached home, there was tremendous shock in Comber. Local people felt it would be right to erect a memorial to Thomas, and so the Andrews Memorial Hall was built on the Ballygowan Road, just opposite the spinning mill and not far from his birthplace at Ardara. Thomas' young daughter Elizabeth cut the first sod in 1913, and in 1914 his mother laid a memorial stone. The hall officially opened in 1915 and for many years served as a community hall.

Thomas Andrews was a staunch Unionist, and, like most of the people of Comber, completely opposed to the proposed introduction of Home Rule. When Sir Edward Carson established the Ulster Volunteer Force to defend the Union, thousands answered the call. Thomas' brother John Miller

The UVF in 1914 outside Cuan on the Killinchy Road. Cuan, now Eusemere, was the home of Captain George Bruce, the Company commander, who drilled his men in the Lower Distillery yard. He is standing front left.

The frail features of a brave man. Edmund de Wind VC, killed in action, March 1918. De Wind Drive is named after him.

Andrews became a commander in Comber West Company of the UVF. Indeed a roll call of Comber men who enlisted would reveal many names well known in the area. George Bruce was another company commander. He was managing director of the distillery, of which his father was chairman, and he drilled his men in the Lower Distillery yard.

'Carson's army' never took up arms against the state. For when Britain became involved in war with Kaiser Bill's Germany in 1914, the UVF was incorporated into the British army as the 36th (Ulster) Division, showing where their true loyalties lay. 426 men from Comber and district answered the call to arms. Two of Comber's ministers enlisted as chaplains. One was Charles Campbell Manning, rector of St. Mary's Parish Church from 1911-18. The other was Thomas McConnell of Second Presbyterian Church, who emigrated to Canada after the war.

During the course of the war seventy-nine Comber men made the supreme sacrifice. On 1st July 1916, the 36th Division was decimated at the Somme. John and Mary Donaldson of Comber received devastating news. Their three sons, Sammy, Jimmy and John, had all been killed in action on that terrible day. George Bruce was another who never made it back. He was killed on 2nd October 1918 in Flanders, just about six weeks before the Armistice. His name lives on in Bruce Avenue.

Another Comber hero, Edmund de Wind, is remembered in De Wind Drive on the same housing estate. He was the only Comber man to win the Victoria Cross. De Wind was born in Comber in 1883, the son of Arthur de Wind, chief engineer on the Belfast and County Down Railway, and for many years organist at St. Mary's Parish Church. In 1911 de Wind moved to Canada, and when war broke out, he enlisted in the Canadian Expeditionary Force. However in 1917 he transferred to the 36th (Ulster) Division.

In early 1918 Edmund's regiment was in Picardy in France. He took up position at Racecourse Redoubt near the village of Grugies, unaware of the fierce German offensive that was about to begin. One of the first lines of resistance the Germans met was at the Racecourse Redoubt, and for seven hours De Wind held his post practically single-handed, although twice wounded. He continued to repel attack after attack until he was killed.[4] After the war, a captured German field gun was presented to the people of Comber in his memory. This gun sat proudly in Comber Square until the Second

World War, when it was taken away for recycling. Fortunately, the metal inscription plates were preserved and can be seen in the porch of the parish church.

Comber's war memorial was unveiled in 1923, and the dead are still remembered every year on the first of July and on Remembrance day. What sort of world had they given their lives for?

Sacrilege? The de Wind field gun being cut up for scrap in the early years of the Second World War.

10 Between the wars

Moneyrea for baps and tay, Ballygowan for brandy,
Magherascouse for pigs and coos, but Cummer is my dandy.

The anonymous author of these lines is right to wax lyrical about our little town. We don't appreciate or celebrate it half enough. However, even the most enthusiastic Comberian would have to admit that the place was a bit of a backwater in the period between the wars. So this might be the time to mention the alternative view: 'when God made Comber, he had nothing else to make'. The 1925 *Belfast and Ulster Directory* gives us an interesting glimpse of its life and its people at this time.

Comber's farmers receive high praise as being 'amongst the most industrious, enlightened and prosperous in Ireland'. At their head, as ever, were the Andrews family, who farmed almost a thousand acres of agricultural land and employed 535 people in the spinning mill. Other industries included the Albion stitching factory, the nut and bolt factory of Messrs. Wishart & Co., and the New Comber Gas Company owned by T.D. Hamilton. By 1925 our local Gas Works had some four to five hundred customers and maintained an average output of ten million cubic feet. Profitable contracts were secured for by-products like coke, tar and spent oxides. However, the coming of electricity was to prove fatal. Production collapsed after 1925, and in 1957 the company closed.

It wasn't all gloom and doom. The Upper Distillery was rebuilt in Scrabo stone in the early 1920s at a cost of fifty thousand pounds. It became the

The distillery cooperage, where the barrels were made. Many a hangover is lurking in these casks, dated 1925, Old Comber's centenary year.

most up-to-date distillery in Ireland. All the latest machinery was installed and the manufacturing process became entirely automatic. Barrels were made across the street in the cooperage, on premises now occupied by Comber Commercial Centre. The coopers were the distillery's best-paid staff, receiving five shillings and seven pence (28p) a day in 1908. Women in the bottling plant only got two shillings (10p).[1]

The Post, Telegraph and Stamp Office was in Mill Street. Miss Patterson was postmistress until 1935 when her sister Mrs. Smyth took over. Beside the post office was R.J. White's. 'Mickey' White would try a hand at anything which turned over a bob or two. With the help of Jim Barry, he catered for weddings and other functions, and provided musicians for dances at venues like the Andrews Hall. He also brought picture shows to the Andrews Hall in the 1920s. These must have been an incredible experience. Movies were silent then, with a piano belting out an accompaniment to the flickering images. On Saturdays the children's matinee was two-pence (less than $1/2$p)! And at Christmas time the youngsters were given a bag of sweets on their way in. However, a real picture house was needed, and a suitable building was found in Castle Street in the form of the long sloping stables of the Old House. Money was spent and the stables were magically transformed into a cinema with white art deco facade. The interior walls were exotically painted

Mickey White's shop in Mill Street. Mickey is on the right. Oh to step back in time and peruse the items displayed in the window! Mickey also brought the 'flicks' to Comber.

in a style not unlike Chinese willow pattern. The cinema opened in January 1934 with *King Kong*. A roaring good start![2]

The RUC station, occupied by Sergeants Collins and Gilmore, was in Mill Street (now Castle Street). This part of the Street was known as Barrack Row. The barracks had a rather low doorway, and you can imagine the tall policemen taking many a bang on the head as they tried to enter. Later the police moved to better premises further down the street, under the arch beside what is now the Breadmill bakery. The police station is now in Killinchy Street. Sergeant Edwards, who came to Comber in 1936, lived in the Old House (style indeed!). Later, during the 1950s, one of his successors, Sergeant Killick, organised boxing tournaments in the Andrews Hall. The Petty Sessions were also held here, on the last Monday of the month. The Northern Banking Company committed to the town by running a proper bank in the Square, but the Ulster Bank just stuck a toe in the water, running an agency in Castle Street, open only on Tuesdays.

The Customs and Excise office, connected with the distillery, was in Killinchy Street, while there was a telephone call office in the Square run by Maude Porter. Three doctors are listed, including, somewhat unusually for those days, a lady, Margaret Nelson; as is a veterinary surgeon (F.R.

V.E. Day 1945. Note the air raid shelter.

inscribed on two pillars. These were replaced in 1995 when the Square was re-designed, and the plaques were transferred to the new pillars. Many regarded the 1995 facelift as an act of vandalism, looking on in horror as a number of beautiful trees were axed. For a while the Square looked a mess as large machines devoured the trees, converting them into bark chippings for re-use. At the same time the flowerbeds were torn asunder to make way for the 'new look'. It was a great relief when the job was completed, and today the Square remains an impressive feature of the town. Gillespie would have been delighted with his new spotlights.

Comber celebrated the coronation of Elizabeth II in 1953 with huge enthusiasm. Many would have remembered the day seven years previously (March 19th 1946) when the then Princess Elizabeth came to our little town. The occasion was a baptism in the Parish Church. Her Royal Highness was godmother to baby Elizabeth Lavinia Sarah King, daughter of Ozzie and Patsy King, her Lady in Waiting.

All aboard the Coronation Special in 1953. Note Comber's own Queen Elizabeth raising a gloved hand centre right. Doesn't she do that wave to perfection? Anyone recognise themselves?

But such glamorous occasions have been rare. During the last fifty years Comber has become a dormitory town, with workers travelling to Belfast, Newtownards and other places. It has little native industry or commerce, the only remaining large factory being that of Airsteps on the Newtownards Road, which makes carpet underlay. Gone are the distilleries, victims of changing tastes and lack of financial backing in what became a specialised, highly competitive industry. The Lower Distillery closed in the 1930s and has since been demolished. The Upper Distillery struggled to break even, and a daring theft of spirits out through the roof didn't help. The last distilling of the now fabled Old Comber Whiskey took place in 1952. The buildings were later converted into a small trading complex. At the time of writing the distillery still stands. There are plans to develop housing on the site, but thankfully the chimney is to be retained as a reminder of the past.

Gone too is the spinning mill, which in latter years had been importing flax from Belgium to produce linen yarn. In 1997 the machines fell silent, the chimneys stopped smoking and the gates shut for the last time. It was no longer an economically viable proposition. The closure came as a great shock.

But the fine old building will hopefully survive. There are plans to create a village of luxury apartments complete with swimming pool on the site. The Andrews family have not completely cut their links with linen. Johnnie Andrews has recently opened a mail order business based at the Clattering Ford on the Ballygowan Road, selling Irish Linen and things like Aran sweaters. Products include table linen identical to that used on the *Titanic*.

Not the Blitz. The Darragh Road in 1987, during the demolition of the Orlit houses. Had they not been knocked down, they would probably have fallen.

Today Comber boasts around ten thousand inhabitants, a fourfold increase over the 1951 population. Housing estates were built to cope with this expansion, and the town has grown in all directions. The 1950s saw the McCormick and De Wind Estates built along the Newtownards Road, and then in the 1960s the Copelands and Dermott estates on what was once the 'forty acre'. Developments have also sprung up out the Glen and Old Ballygowan Roads, and at Carnesure off the Killinchy Road. Many of the 'Orlit' houses built in 1951 proved unstable, and the whole area around Darragh Road has had to be rebuilt. Accommodation for our senior citizens has been provided at Mount Alexander and the Four Seasons nursing homes, while the Presbyterian Housing Association has built sheltered accommodation at Stepping Stones in Bridge Street, and Weir Court off High Street. It is worth noting that many of the stories and anecdotes in this book were gleefully divulged to us by these old friends, whose memories span most of the last century.

More schools have opened. The Secondary School in Darragh Road dates from 1957. The first headmaster was Harold Cameron, who had been head of Comber Elementary School. This now became Comber Primary with Norman Nevin as headmaster. In the 1970s a second primary school started in the Andrews Memorial Hall, moving next door to its present location in 1978. Comber Library, opened in 1967, has been another huge boon to the town, as is the Early Learning Centre in Park Way. The latter is also the home of Comber Historical Society, formed in 2000. The town also boasts its own leisure centre. However, a modern community hall in the centre of the town, suitable for the use of all age groups, is badly needed.

Additional accommodation and facilities have thankfully been accompanied by improved sanitation. An £150,000 sewage plant was built in 1958 at Ballyrickard on the shores of Strangford Lough, and gradually the last dry toilets in the town were replaced by the latest plumbed WCs. The pumps and street fountains gave way to a piped water supply in 1957. Flooding remained a problem in Bridge Street until the early 1980s, when a major scheme was carried out on the Inler. The scheme involved widening the bridge and reinforcing the riverbank. It was a great success. One victim of the renovations was a small concrete structure which had housed a water ram, once used to flush water to the toilets at the primary school. Hopefully the toilets still flush!

One consequence of the drainage works was an endless queue of traffic on the Newtownards Road. Such queues are now a daily occurrence. Our roads are grossly overcrowded. Valiant efforts have been made in recent years to have the railway to Belfast restored. Much of the track bed is still intact. The latest thinking is that an 'e-way' could be constructed along this, on which special buses would run from Comber into the heart of Belfast. In addition, work has just commenced on Phase Two of the Comber by-pass (Phase One was opened in 1962 between the Belfast and Killinchy Roads). This will extend the present by-pass out to the Newtownards Road and thus ease traffic congestion, at least for a while.[1] Thankfully, a plan to build a new so-called 'village' at Camperdown, between Comber and Dundonald, has been abandoned.

One man who could often be seen striding along the road to Dundonald was 'Wee' Willie Brown, at four foot eight inches (1.4 metres) the smallest

Wee Willie Brown, at four foot eight inches (1.42 metres) the smallest postie in Ireland. Those short legs travelled many long miles in their day.

postman in Ireland. He made all deliveries on foot, walking an estimated 131,712 miles between 1916-48![2] Willie's girlfriend lived in Dundonald. He always carried his big mailbag over his back when visiting her. On these occasions it did not contain mail, but rather some bricks – to stand on when ready for a good 'coort'!

Comber has always had its share of characters. Willie Graham in High Street made blackthorn sticks. And then there was Joe Blake from Newtownards, who had swum the North Channel, and could often be seen in Comber. He was instantly recognisable by his long, stringy hair, large boots and swirling skirt. He maintained that he would continue to dress in this way until women stopped wearing trousers. No one knows what was in the large shopping bag he always carried. And Ottilie Patterson, a famous jazz and blues singer, was born in Comber in 1932. During the 1950s she was vocalist with the Chris Barber Band, and in 1959 she married Barber.

Comber's state-of-the-art cinema opened in 1957, showing all the latest blockbusters.

Not only people have character. Buildings also develop a certain charisma. In 1956 the now dilapidated and rather spooky Old House was demolished to make way for a modern cinema seating four hundred people. For a time the old Picture House also continued to operate, and until it closed there was a choice of twelve movies per week. Large crowds queued out onto Castle Street for the major blockbusters. Bikes were stashed in Tommy Murphy's yard. But television and then video dealt fatal blows to Comber Cinema, which was finally flattened by a large crane and ball in June 1985. Wellworths bought the site, and gave Comber its very own shopping centre. In April 1986 a queue of expectant shoppers amassed outside the new store. The doors were unlocked, and the town's very first trolley-wielding punters stormed the brand new shiny displays. Comber's latest trading post was in business.

The cinema has gone. But the movies are not dead around Comber, thanks to two brothers, Roy and Noel Spence. Both were great movie buffs, and by the 1970s Roy was earning a reputation for making extremely competent horror and sci-fi films. In 1974 Noel opened his own Tudor Cinema beside his home on the Drumhirk Road, and Comber's newest moviehouse flickered into life.

We all have our favourite memories of Comber. For some it may be going to feed the swans up at the dam. Others will remember Duffy's circus. Or

Comber's conquering heroes. The Rec. football team that lifted the Steel & Sons Cup on Christmas Day, 1991.

what about Davy's chip shop in Bridge Street, where you were always given a few samples while you waited? Who could have imagined the number of fast food shops that would open in the town, including some offering Chinese and Indian meals? Did you take part in the wheelie bin races of Comber Civic Week, or purchase one of that mass of paper 'boats' that came floating down the Inler in the duck derby? Football fans will recall Comber Rec.'s finest hour on Christmas Day 1991 when they beat Brantwood 4-1 in the final of the Steel & Sons Cup. They have twice since made it to the final, only to fall at the last hurdle. Incidentally, when the Rec. were formed sometime around 1950, they played in the Churches League. This meant that they had to affiliate to a church, and so the team attended bible class at First Comber, which for some was no small shock to the system.

Another remarkable sporting achievement is that of David Calvert and Martin Miller from Comber Rifle Club, winners at the 2002 Commonwealth Games in the full bore pairs shooting event. David also won the gold medal in the singles event, bringing his tally of Commonwealth medals to four golds and three bronze.

The last few years have seen a number of anniversaries in our churches. Both the Non-subscribing and Second Comber celebrated 150 years between 1988 and 1990.[3] And 1995 saw the 350th anniversary of First Comber. The

Provocative porch. The porch of the Methodist Church in Bridge Street, left standing after the rest of the building was unceremoniously flattened in 1995.

formation of the congregation was remembered by a special service commencing in St. Mary's, the mother church, followed by a procession up to First Comber. In that same year the Methodist Church disappeared almost overnight. The structure was apparently unsound, and the JCB's were called in. The congregation continues to meet in the hall. Other churches have sprung up in recent years. The Baptists meet on the site of the old gasworks, Comber Christian Centre is in Mill Street, the Brethren are on the Belfast Road and the Free Presbyterians on the Newtownards Road, just beside the old Glassmoss level crossing.

The Roman Catholic church sadly suffered damage from an incendiary device in 1993, and after refurbishment was re-dedicated that July. It has to be said however that, although Comber is a town with staunch loyalist traditions, there is a generally harmonious relationship between protestants and Catholics. Comber has been less affected by the Troubles than many other places, although a number of members of the security forces from the town lost their lives during the conflict. And it was nearby at La Mon House in 1978 that one of the worst atrocities of the last thirty years occurred, when the Provisional IRA murdered twelve people and badly injured twenty-three in a firebomb attack on the crowded restaurant.

Comber Square from the tower of St. Mary's.

Comber is changing. The heart of the old town is still there, but regeneration is much needed to help the ailing business community and to counter the negative affects of decades of sprawl. Many shops and commercial properties lie empty, and manufacturing is virtually extinct. The Spinning Mill has closed. The Albion factory has been demolished, as has the Thompson Hall. The Upper Distillery complex will shortly go the same way.

This may all sound somewhat depressing. But there is much to be optimistic about. The former car showrooms in the Square, having lain derelict for several months, have got a reprieve, and are once more occupied. There are plans to convert the building into shops and town housing. Our suburbs may be bland but they are pleasant, and the old town retains much of its charm. It is to be hoped that the recent very welcome revival of the tradition of living in the centre of the town will continue. However, we hope that wherever possible, old buildings will be re-used, new development will be tasteful, and that, on completion of the by-pass, people will be encouraged to come into the town centre and use the local facilities again. And surely there must be potential for tourism in what is a beautiful and historic area. A small museum would be nice, focusing on topics such as linen, whiskey, potatoes and the railway.

Today there is a great re-awakening of interest in the history of our province, especially at local level. We would like to think that our past will be preserved for coming generations to enjoy, and that in years to come people will still be able to say, as did the poet of old, that 'Cummer is my dandy'.

The townlands of Comber parish

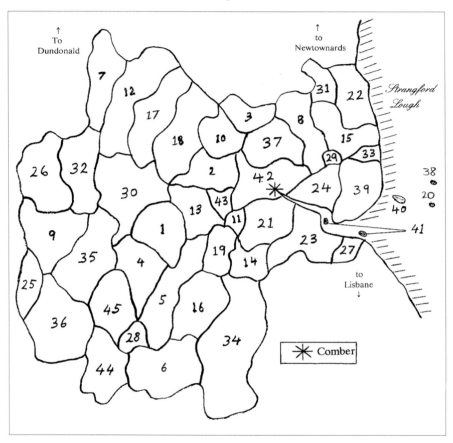

The civil parish of Comber is quite a large entity. It extends northwards almost to Dundonald, and westwards to incorporate Crossnacreevy and Moneyreagh. It runs eastwards into Strangford Lough, encompassing several of the Lough's islands, and southwards to include Ballygowan.

1. Ballyalloly
2. Ballyaltikilligan
3. Ballyalton
4. Ballybeen
5. Ballycreelly
6. Ballygowan
7. Ballyhanwood
8. Ballyhenry
9. Ballykeel
10. Ballyloghan
11. Ballymagaughey
12. Ballymaglaff
13. Ballymalady
14. Ballynichol
15. Ballyrickard
16. Ballyrush
17. Ballyrussell
18. Ballystockart
19. Ballywilliam
20. Black Island
21. Carnasure
22. Castleavery
23. Cattogs
24. Cherryvalley
25. Clontonakelly
26. Crossnacreevy
27. Cullintraw
28. Edenslate
29. Glassmoss
30. Gransha
31. Killynether
32. Lisleen
33. Longlands
34. Magherascouse
35. Moneyreagh
36. Monlough
37. Mount Alexander
38. Ogilby Island
39. Ringcreevy
40. Rough Island
41. Salt Marsh Islands
42. Townparks
43. Trooperfield
44. Tullygarvan
45. Tullyhubbert

Notes

1 Back to our roots

1. The Ordnance Survey renders the name Enler. But we have adopted the local spelling.

3 Two Combers

1. The third viscount had a peculiar medical condition. Owing to an accident as a child, an abscess had formed on his left side. This was covered with a silver plate, and when this was removed his heart could be seen beating. He was examined by Dr. William Harvey, the man who discovered the circulation of the blood. Harvey must have found Montgomery an exceptionally interesting patient.

4 No mean village

1. The Muster Roll of that year mentions a 'Thomas Andrew – Sword and Musket', and a 'Robert Andrew – Sword and Snaphance'. A snaphance was a superior type of musket, and so an indication of relative wealth.

2. The Upper Mill was on the site of Comber Christian Centre, formerly the Laureldale Hall. The other mill, the Old Mill, was by the banks of the Inler, beside the all-weather hockey pitch, and remained there until fairly recently.

3. Thomas's name is carved on one of the entrance pillars to the grounds of St. Mary's Parish Church, along with that of James Lemont of Gransha. Both men were churchwardens and paid for erection of the pillars.

6 Money, whiskey, linen and sweat

1. John's son Marcus later founded the important printing and publishing business of Marcus Ward & Co. in Belfast.

2. James died in 1841, shortly after taking ill while chairing a Unitarian meeting in First Rosemary Street Church, Belfast.

8 Molly's world

1. There was however a connection between John Miller and the Andrews family. Miller had married a daughter of Lord Pirrie. Later, in 1870, Thomas Andrews of Ardara married Eliza Pirrie, the niece of Miller's wife. Their eldest son was John Miller Andrews.

2. Later, William Cochrane is listed as a threshing machine proprietor at the same site.

3. A totem pole was erected at Island Hill as a cultural link with Canada and its migrating birds.

4. In exchange he gave the distillery the dam where Second Comber Presbyterian Church now have their car park. This was once known as Taylor's Dam, presumably taking its name from David Taylor, a nineteenth century minister of Second Comber.

9 A town mourns

1. Some tenants thought they could do better by taking their case to the newly formed land courts. But here they experienced infinite delays, possibly because Lord Londonderry, as head of the Irish government, was in a position to make things difficult for them. This strategy proved successful. In 1890 the courts reduced the rents of applicants by twenty-five per cent.

2. Canon George Smyth of St. Mary's Church of Ireland appears on their banner. He was a great benefactor to the poor and needy. In 1913 a transept was added to the church in his memory.

3. Had Miss McDowell lived another hundred and ten years, she could have been buried closer to home. Land has recently been procured on the Ballygowan Road for another cemetery.

4. Edmund de Wind has no known grave, and his name appears on the Poziers Memorial to the missing in France.

10 Between the wars

1. Second Comber Church car park marks the site of the Upper Distillery dam. A concrete structure still in existence, known as 'The Troughs', conveyed water to the dam from the Glen River.

2. Things did not always run smoothly. A reel of film could often be put on upside down, yet the Indians somehow never fell off their horses unless they were shot, in which case they mysteriously went upwards.

11 Within living memory

1. The late James Miskelly recalled a proposal for a by-pass in 1936. It would have cut from Lower Crescent, along the right hand side of the Inler, and out to the

Belfast Road. Later development would make this venture impossible today.

2. In 1946 the Post Office moved to the Square with Mrs Smyth as post-mistress. After a period in Bridge Street, it is now in Castle Street, although mail deliveries today come direct from Newtownards.

3. Second Comber unveiled a plaque in the loft in Milling's yard at the bottom of High Street where the congregation had first met. This has been re-sited on the church premises.

Bibliography

Belfast and Northern Ireland Directory 1948

Belfast and Ulster Directory 1925

Centenary 1877-1977 St. Patrick's Church, Newtownards (1977)

Comber & District War Memorial – Order of service for unveiling and dedication ceremony 14th April 1923; ditto *27th June 1952*

Comber Distilleries Co. Ltd. Centenary Year 1825-1925 (Souvenir booklet, 1925)

Down and Connor Historical Society Journal 1936

Londonderry Estate Papers *(PRONI, D.654, D.714)*

Newtownards Chronicle

Northern Star

Parliamentary Gazetteer of Ireland 1845

Pigot's Directory 1824

Poor Law Enquiry 1836

Post Office Directory Belfast 1843

St. Mary's Parish Church, souvenir brochure of the New Hall (1983)

These Three Hundred Years 1645-1945 and Twenty-Five More: First Comber Presbyterian Church (1970)

Ulster Vintage Car Club Book of the Ards T.T. (Belfast, 1978)

Andrews, S. *Nine Generations, A History of the Andrews Family of Comber, Co. Down* (Belfast, 1958)

Bardon, J. *A History of Ulster* (Belfast, 1992)

Bassett, G.H. *County Down, Guide and Directory* (Dublin, 1886)

Brett, C.E.B. *Buildings of North County Down* (Belfast, 2002)

Brown, R. *Strangford Lough* (Belfast, 1990)

Bullock, S.F. *Thomas Andrews* (London, 1912; reprinted Belfast, 1999)

Carr, P. *The Most Unpretending of Places* (Dundonald, 1987)

Clarke, R.S.J. *Gravestone Inscriptions, Volume 5 (Co Down)* (Belfast, 1984)

Coakham, D. *Belfast & County Down Railway* (Leicester, 1998)

Cooney, D.L. *The Methodists in Ireland* (Dublin, 2001)

Crookshank, C.H. *History of Methodism in Ireland* (Belfast & London, 1885)

Day, A. & McWilliams, P. *Ordnance Survey Memoirs of Ireland: Parishes of Co. Down II, North Down and the Ards* (Belfast, 1991)

Duffin, A. Reminiscences of Comber, its inhabitants and our life there *(PRONI, T.3023)*

Frame, Rev. Wm. & Marshall Mrs E. *A History of Comber Non-Subscribing Presbyterian Church* (1988)

Green, E.R.R. *Industrial Archaeology of Co. Down* (Belfast, 1963)

Griffiths, R. *Valuation of tenements* (Dublin, 1861)

Haines, K. *North Down Memories* (Belfast, 2000)

Harper, W. O. *A History of Second Presbyterian Church Comber 1838-1990* (Belfast 1992)

Harris, W. *The Antient and Present State of the County of Down* (Dublin, 1744)

Hill, G. (ed.) *Montgomery Manuscripts* (Belfast, 1869)

Hill, M., Turner, B. & Dawson, K. *1798: Rebellion in County Down* (Newtownards, 1998)

Holmes, F. *The Presbyterian Church in Ireland* (Dublin, 2000)

Jope, E.M. *Archaeological Survey of Co. Down* (Belfast, 1966)

Kennedy, M.L. & McNeill, D.B. *Early Bus Services in Ulster* (Belfast, 1997)

Kinealy, C. & Parkhill,T. (eds) *The Famine in Ulster* (Belfast, 1997)

Kirkpatrick, N. *Take a Second Look* (Comber, 1993)

Knox, A. *History of the County of Down* (Dublin, 1875)

Leslie, J.B. & Swanzy, H.B. *Biographical Succession Lists, Diocese of Down* (1936)

Lewis, S. *Topographical Dictionary of Ireland* (London, 1837)

Lyttle, W.G. *Betsy Gray or Hearts of Down* (Newcastle, 1968)

Mallory, J.P. & McNeill, T.E. *The Archaeology of Ulster* (Belfast, 1991)

McCavery, T. *Newtown, A History of Newtownards* (Dundonald, 1994)

McNeill, T.E. *Anglo-Norman Ulster* (Edinburgh, 1980)

McRoberts, F.M. *Memoirs of Evenings in the Square*

Nevin, N. The Story of Comber (Comber library, unpublished)

O'Laverty, J. *The Diocese of Down and Connor* (Dublin, 1880)

Patterson, E.M. *The Belfast & County Down Railway* (Newton Abbot, 1982)

Reeves, W. *Ecclesiastical Antiquities* (Dublin, 1867)

Robb, W. *Journal of Irish Railway Society, Vol. 19, No. 130 (June 1996);* 'Comber as a Railway Centre'

Stevenson, J. *Two Centuries of Life in Down 1600-1800* (Belfast, 1920; reprinted Dundonald, 1990)

Stewart, A.T.Q. *The Summer Soldiers* (Belfast, 1995)

Stone, G. Diary (PRONI, D.626)

Townsend, B. *The Lost Distilleries of Ireland* (Glasgow, 1997, 1999)

Wakeham, E. *The Bravest Soldier, Sir Rollo Gillespie* (Edinburgh & London, 1937)

Wilsdon, B. *The Sites of the 1798 Rising in Antrim and Down* (Belfast, 1997)

Wildfowl and Wetlands Trust Centre *Castle Espie, A Short History*

Index

Adair, John 96

Adventurer 95

Affreca 22

Air Raid Precautions 99

Airsteps factory 52, 102

Albalanda 23

Albion factory 88, 108

Allen, Dr. 57

Allen, James George 76

American troops 72, 99

Andrew, abbot of Cummor 24

Andrews family 37, 58, 60, 69, 73, 88, 99; Robert (1630), 112; Thomas (1630), 112; Thomas, miller of Comber 37, 38; John 'the great' 38-43, 50, 58; Thomas (b. 1727) 38, 39, 112; James of Uraghamore 41-43, 50, 54, 61, 112; John, agent of Lord Londonderry 50, 51, 53, 54, 61, 69, 71-73, 94; William Glenny 50, 54, 71, 72; Thomas (1798-1838) 51; Isaac 50-52,74; Margaret 71; Mary 71; James of Carnesure 71; John (1838-1903) 71; Thomas of Ardara 64, 71, 72, 74 , 85, 113; Fanny 71, 80; John, son of Isaac 74; John Miller 85, 86, 99, 113; Thomas, shipbuilder 84, 85, 99; Thomas, the cooper 38; James, Lord Chief Justice 92; Willie, cricketer 94; Elizabeth 85; John Ormrod 99; Johnnie 103; bleach green 18, 39, 51, 73, 94; burial vault 36, 72; Memorial Hall 68, 85, 89, 90, 104; spinning mill 51, 54, 66, 72-75, 82, 83, 85, 88, 99, 100, 102, 103, 108

Arcot 48

Ardara 85

Ardmillan 68

Armagh 18

Artillery, first use in Ireland 24

Artt, Billy 96

Ashdown, Paddy 72

Augustinians 21

Aureen 75, 93

Ayrshire 26

Ballybeen House 32

Ballydrain Road 15, 28, 77

Ballygowan 63, 66, 88; Road 21, 66, 72, 84, 85, 103, 113; Old Ballygowan Road 103

Ballygraffan 18

Ballyhenry Road 67

Ballyloughan 18

Ballymacarrett 68

Ballymena 39, 79

Ballynahinch 44

Ballynichol Road 17, 18

Ballyrickard 24, 104

Ballystockart 18

Ballywilliam 99

Baltic tanks 66

Bangor 24, 28

Banks 77: Northern 90; Ulster 90

Barnhill 59, 64, 82

Barns, Mr. 44

Barrack Row 90

Barrington, William 46

Barry Street 52, 55

Barry, Jim 89
Barry's Inn 54
Bassett, G.H. 18, 77
Bath 45
Battletown 30
Beetling mill 39
Belfast 38, 42, 59, 63, 64, 68, 72, 74, 77, 84, 98, 99, 102, 104; Road 24, 64, 98, 107, 114
Belfast and County Down Railway (BCDR) 63, 64, 67, 68, 86
Belgium 102
Benedictines 22
Bengal 49
Bennett, Edmund 32
Bernard, Peter 54
Big House, the 41, 50, 71
Binning, John 31
Black Bob 48
Black Death 24
Blake, Joe 105
Blathewic 22
Boxing 90
Boyne 32
Braeside 83
Braidstane 26
Brantwood 106
Breadly, Sam 35
Breadmill bakery 90
Breakey, Rev. J.C. 91
Bridge Street 24, 42, 82, 95, 96, 103, 104, 106, 107, 114
British Legion 92
Bronze Age 18
Brown, James 32
Brown, Wee Willie 104, 105
Browne, Captain 25
Browne, Dave 99
Brownlow Street 75
Bruce Avenue 86
Bruce, Edward 24
Bruce, George James 82, 85, 86
Bruce, Samuel 75
Byrne, William 51

Cairns, James 60
Cairns, Tommy 67

Calvert, David 106
Cameron, Harold 104
Camperdown 104
Canada 58, 77, 86, 113
Candle making 39
Car park 18, 20, 57, 69, 70, 76
Carmarthenshire 23
Carnesure 40, 103
Carrickfergus castle 26
Carson, Sir Edward 85
Castle Espie 76, 77
Castle Lane 20, 27, 74, 76, 94
Castle Street 38, 39, 41, 58, 64, 65, 71, 89, 90, 94, 95, 105, 114
Castlebeg 24, 51
Castlereagh, Viscount 60
Catha Dun, Brian 22
Catholic emancipation 82
Celts 15, 18
Cemetery 84, 113
Cess 34
Chambers, Jack 98
Chantrey, Sir Francis 49
Charles II 30, 31
Cherryvalley 37, 45
Chetwynd, Lieutenant 44
Chris Barber Band 105
Churches:
    Baptist Church 40, 58, 107; Black (Augustinian) abbey 21, 24; Brethren 107; Celtic monastery 19, 20; Church of Scots settlers 26, 51, 60; Cistercian abbey 22-27; Comber Christian Centre 107, 112; First Presbyterian 30-34, 36, 42, 44, 54, 55, 60-62, 79, 80, 91, 106, 107; Free Presbyterian 107; League 106; Methodist 42, 107; Roman Catholic 18, 77, 79, 107; Second Presbyterian 51, 61, 62, 80, 86, 91, 106, 113, 114; St. Mary's Church of Ireland 22, 23,27, 30, 34-37, 44, 47, 52, 55-57, 60, 72, 86, 91, 101, 107, 108, 112, 113; Unitarian (Non-Subscribing) 51, 60-62,74, 91, 94, 106; Presbyterian Housing Association 103; Revival of 1859 62, 79
Cinema and movies 71, 89, 90, 105, 113; Tudor Cinema 105

Cistercians 22, 23, 26
Cists 18
Civil War 30
Claneboye 25, 26
Claneboye, Viscount – see Hamilton
Clarke 44
Clattering Ford 103
Close, Father 77
Cochrane, William 113
Collins, Sergeant 90
Colvil, Sir Robert 31, 37
Comber: building of canal at 59; by pass 63, 68, 104, 109, 113; Christianity comes to 19; Civic Week 106; Coterie 42; Cruising Club 34; drainage scheme in 104; emigration from 58, 73; Fair days in 54, 57, 83; Famine, effects of 58; First motor car in 76; Gas Company 58, 88, 107; Historical Society 104; housing in 55, 56, 103; industry in 18, 37, 39, 40, 50-52, 58, 67, 72-77, 88, 89, 102, 108; Letter of 1688 31; medieval drainage system 23, 24; origin of name 16; pier near 59; policing in 52, 54, 77, 90, 100; politics in 42, 43, 81, 107; population of 33, 84, 103; poverty in 35, 42, 56-58; Rifle Club 106; Scots settlement of 26-30; sewage in 56, 84, 104; Sports Centre 42; street lighting in 58, 84; tourism 109; traffic chaos in 104; Troubles, effect of 107; water supply 104; Commercial Centre 89; Leisure Centre 72, 104; Library 104
Comber River 15, 16, 40, 59, 95
Commonwealth Games 106
Conla 19
Coo Vennel 31
Cooke, Dr. Henry 62
Cooperage 89
Copelands estate 103
Corbitt, Mary 39
Cork 46
Corken, Tom 66, 95, 97
Cormac, abbot of Comar 21
Cow Lane 31
Cricket: North Down Cricket Club 18, 19, 39, 93, 94; M.C.C. 94
Cromwell, Oliver 30
Crosby, Tommy 68

Crossan, Willie 95
Cuan 85
Cuming, Mr. 43
Cummer Ann (Maxwell) 91
Cunningham, Robert 32, 33, 42
Customs and Excise 33, 52, 75, 90

Darini 18
Darragh Road 18, 92, 103, 104
Davidson, Sammy 68
Davies, Rev. James Glynne 91
Davy's chip shop 106
De Courcy, John 21, 22
De Mandevilles 24
De Rossal, Ralph 21
De Wind: Drive and estate 86, 103; Arthur 86; Edmund 82, 86, 87, 113
Dermott estate 103
Derry/Londonderry 31
Distilleries – see whiskey distilling
Doherty, William Hugh 62
Donaghadee 63, 64, 67
Donaldson family 86
Dowdall, William 31
Down, County 18, 21, 24, 25, 43, 79
Downpatrick 31, 59
Drennan, Dr. William, 54; Molly 69-72, 75-78, 80; Sarah 54, 71
Drogheda 40
Druid's Altar 18
Drumhirk Road 105
Drumlins 15
Dublin 32, 40, 45, 81
Duck derby 106
Duck Hole View 73
Dufferin, Lady 50
Duffy's circus 105
Dunbar, George 66, 68
Dunbar, Maggie Ann 94
Dundonald 32, 91, 97, 104, 105
Dunkerly, Rev. Thomas 80

Early Learning Centre 104
Eason's newspaper kiosk 64
Edward VII 76
Edwards, Sergeant 90

Egypt 58
Elizabeth I 25, 26
Elizabeth II, coronation 101, 102; royal visit of
    Princess 101
Elom, Plain of 19
Emain Macha 18
Erasmus Smyth Charity 54, 55
Essex, Earl of 25
Eusemere 85
E-way 104

Fairy field and ring 24
Farming 15, 17, 26, 28, 42, 50, 52-54, 58, 77,
    78, 81, 83, 88, 99; Land, transfer of 81, 113;
    North East Society 54
First Rosemary Street Church 112
Fisher, Robbie 95
Fishing 28
Five Sisters 17, 18
Flanders 86
Flooding 57, 104
Flour mill 40, 51, 62, 74
Football: Comber Amateurs 93; Comber Rec.
    106; Comber Star 93; Steel & Sons Cup 106
Forsythe, Robert 72
Forty acre field 103
Four Seasons nursing home 103
Frame, Dr. James 73
France/French 43, 46, 58, 86, 113
Freemasons 46, 48
Fresall, James 26

Gabbey, Eliza 73
Galway, Thomas 75
Geneva bible 27
George III 45
Georgian houses in Square 37
Germany 86
Ghaist Hole 33, 34, 44, 95
Giant's Grave 18
Gibson, Jacob 70
Gibson, Robert 68
Gillespie: Hugh 43; Monument 23, 45, 47, 48,
57, 78, 101; Sir Robert Rollo 45-49, 51, 78;
Robert Rollo 49
Gilmore, Sergeant 90

Gilpin, Rev. Ian 60
Glassmoss 67, 78, 107
Glebe House 32, 36, 37, 56, 57
Glen River 16, 24, 113
Glen Road 17, 64, 66, 96, 103
Glenny, Frances 42
Gloucestershire 75
Glover, Tommy 99
Gordon, James 30, 31
Graham, Willie 105
Grain store 40, 72, 73
Gransha 112
Greyabbey 22-24
Griffith, John 32
Griffiths, James 96
Grugies 86
Guinney's stones 94
Gullet, the 66

Hadden, Alfred 92
Hall, E.R. 97
Hamilton: James, Viscount Claneboye 26, 28-
30; James, 1st Earl of Clanbrassil 30; Robert,
nephew of Viscount Claneboye 28
Hamilton, John 31
Hamilton, T.D. 88
Hanna, Rev. Robert 80
Harland & Wolff 68, 85
Harris, Walter 36,37, 39
Harvard University 17
Harvey, Dr. William 112
Hen Dung Row 92
Henry VIII 25
Herington, Thomas 32
High Street 31, 55, 62, 67, 82, 91, 95, 103, 105,
114
Hiles, Grace 67
Hill Street 55
Hockey 93
Hoffman kilns 77
Holland 30, 54
Holme, the 92
Holywood 28
Home Guard 99, 100
Home Rule 81, 85
Horner's shop 76

Horse racing 36, 37, 93
House of Industry (poorhouse) 58
Houston, Canon John S. 91
Humphries, Tansey Lee 95

Ice Age 15
Illuminated address 72
Illustrated London News 47, 48
India 48, 49
Inler River 16-18, 24, 52, 53, 59, 104, 106, 112, 113
Iona 68
Irish State Lottery 40
Island Hill 16, 17, 44, 67, 93, 95, 113

Jacobites 32
Jamaica 39
James I 26
Java 48
Jervis, George 71
Jex-Blake, Robert Ferrier 60
Johnston, David John 65
Johnston, George 52
Johnston, William 66
Jones, Rev. James E. 61, 91

Kalunga 48
Kane's of Comber 41, 50, 95
Kelly, Mr. 65
Kennedy, Rev. Gilbert 32
Kennedy, Thomas 29
Kennel Bridge 27, 28
Kildare 45
Kill Combuir 21
Killen, Rev. J.M. 79, 80
Killick, Sergeant 90
Killinchy 24, 30; Road/Street 33, 34, 52, 61, 62, 67, 68, 77, 85, 90, 95, 96, 103, 104
Killynether 24, 60
King Kong 90
King family 101
Kirk, Mrs 100
Knock 92
Knocknagoney 59

La Mon House 107

Laureldale 68, 112
Lemont, James 112
Lindsey, William 71, 80
Linen 38, 39, 50, 51, 72, 82, 102, 103, 109
Lockart, John 29
London 49, 81
Londonderry family 53: First Marquess 37, 43; Lady, wife of Second Marquess 54; Third Marquess 16, 54, 56-58, 62, 72; Sixth Marquess 76, 81, 113
Lower Crescent 59, 77, 91, 92, 95, 113
Lundy, Mr 95
Lurgan, Lord 75

MacDonald, James 94; MacDonald, John A. 95
Magherascouse 88
Mahee Island 20, 25, 37
Mall, the 43
Manning, Rev. Charles Campbell 86
Manor court 54
Marbles 93
Market House 54, 77; Street 77
Mason's marks 23, 28
Master McGra 75, 96
Maxwell Court 21, 60
Maxwell, James 32
McBurney, Andrew 35
McBurney's Row 74
McCance (distillery) 75
McCance, Rev. John 54, 58, 60, 61
McConnell, Rev. Thomas 86
McConnell, Willie 65
McCormick estate 103
McDonald, Thomas 96
McDonald's Corner 96
McDowell, Martha 84, 113
McGowan, Andy 66
McKean, Rev. John 91
McKee, S.W. 91
McLeroth, T. 60
McMillen, Mrs. Robert 96
McNish, Jim 37
McQuillan, Anne 50
McRoberts, F.R. 91
McRoberts, Fannie 96, 100
McRoberts, Thomas 82

McWhinney, Hugh 95
Meerut 48
Megaliths 18
Memorial Gardens 45, 100
Mercat cross 28, 29, 33
Meredith, Isaac of Kilbreght 27
Mesolithic Age 16, 17
Middleton's garage 65
Mill Street 41, 58, 68, 82, 90, 95, 96, 99, 107; View 73
Miller, John 52, 61, 74, 75, 80, 113
Miller, Martin 106
Milling, James 79, 84, 95
Milling's hotel 76; yard 62, 114
Miskelly, James 64, 65, 113
Moate Corner 22
Monastery – see Churches
Moneyreagh 59, 88
Monks' Walk 20
Montgomery, Alexander 54
Montgomery: Hugh, 1st Viscount 26-29; Lady, wife of 1st Viscount 26; Hugh, 2nd Viscount 27, 29, 30; Lady Jean, wife of 2nd Viscount 27, 30, 31; Hugh, 3rd Viscount, 1st Earl of Mount Alexander 30, 112; Hugh, 2nd Earl 31; Henry, 3rd Earl 31; Hugh, 4th Earl 31; Thomas, 5th Earl 31
Morrison, Henry 70
Morrow, Johnnie 96
Mortimer, Rev. Robert 44
Mottes 21, 24
Mount Alexander 17, 30, 31, 42, 93; nursing home 103; Earls of – see Montgomery
Munn, Matthew 95
Murdock, William 52
Murland, Robert 77
Murphy, Tommy 105
Myona 68

Navan Fort 18
Neil, Alex 65, 66
Nelson, Dr. Margaret 90
Nelson, Rev. Isaac 62
Nendrum 20, 22
Neolithic Age 17
Nepal 48

Nevin, Norman 104
New Comber 28, 29, 80
Newbolt, Sir Henry 48
Newcastle 63, 64, 67, 68
Newfoundland 84
Newtown Street 42, 54
Newtownards 22, 24, 28, 59, 63, 83, 92, 95, 97, 98, 102, 105, 114; Amateur Band 47; and Comber Yeomanry 44; Chronicle 78, 83; Road 51, 53, 67, 76, 102-104, 107
Niblock, Mary 96
Night of the big wind 62
Normans 21, 24
North Channel 105
North Down Choral Society 93; Harriers 93
Northern Star 42, 44

O'Denman, Sedna 20
O'Laverty, Rev. J 24
O'Mullegan, John 25
O'Neills 24; Bryan McPhelim 25; Con 26; Henry 24
Oak tree in Castle Street 71, 72
Old Comber whiskey 61, 75, 89, 102
Old Corn Mill 37, 39, 112
Old Cowey 24
Old House, the 38, 41, 42, 57, 69-72, 89, 90, 105
Old Starch mill 72, 73
Olympic 85
Orangeism 32, 64, 81, 82: Comber Old Standard 82; Comber True Blues 82, 113; Comber Ulster Defenders 82; Comber White Flag 82; Goldsprings 82; Orange Hall 32
Ordnance Survey memoir 53
Orlit House 103
Orr, F.J. 91
Orr, Rev. John (First Comber) 32
Orr, Rev. John (Unitarian) 80
Owld Comber 28, 29

Palace Stages 43
Paper mill 51, 53, 57
Park Way 52, 104
Patterson, Ann (Pattie) 89
Patterson, James 52

Patterson, Ottilie 105
Patton, Hugh 96
Petty sessions 90
Philbin, Rev. Dr. 79
Piggery 72, 73
Pirrie family 85, 113
Place, the 69-71
Point to point races 93
Pollock, William 92
Poorhouse Lane 58
Port-au-Prince 46
Porter, Maude 90
Post office 42, 89, 105, 114
Potale Loney 52
Potatoes 15, 26, 54, 109
Pound and Pound Bridge 41
Poziers Memorial 113
Ptolemy 18
Public houses 54; Brownlow Arms 96; First and
    Last 95; Gillespie Arms 96; Murdoch's, Jack
    95; North Down House 64, 96; Railway
    Tavern 96; Simpson's, Alex 96; Tourist
    Trophy lounge 96; Ulster Arms 95

Quarry Corner 97

Racecourse Hill 37
Rachabites 82
Railway 51, 59, 63-68, 94, 98, 104, 109; closure
    of 68; diesel-electric locomotive 63, 67, 68;
    railway station 64, 66-68; signal boxes 65,
    68; Street 66, 68, 96
Ralph Brothers 76
Raphoe, dean of 32
Raven, Thomas 28, 29
Rebellion: of 1641 29; of 1798 43, 44
Reeves, William 20
Regent House School 95
Reid, Robert Rollo 43
Riddle, Alexander 42
Ringcreevy 40
Ringneil 65
Ritchie, Grace 72
Ritchie, John 95
Road maintenance 34, 35, 40, 41
Rodgers, Rev. John 62

Rowan's Stand 98
Royal Ulster Agricultural Society 54

Saintfield 44; Road 35
San Domingo 48
Sandford, surgeon 32
Saran 19
Schomberg 32
Schools and education 77; Andrews Memorial
    104; Barry Street 55; Binning, school run by
    John 31; Comber Elementary/Primary 18, 92,
    104; Comber National School 80, 92; Comber
    Secondary/Intermediate 16, 104; Hibernian
    Society School 55; Londonderry (Erasmus
    Smith) School 47, 54-56, 92; Mill School 73,
    92; Roman Catholic School 77, 78, 92; Smyth
    National School 80, 92; Technical School 41,
    95
Scotland 37, 45
Scrabo: Golf Course 18; Hill 15, 16, 24, 44;
    Sandstone 56, 77, 88; Tower 16
Shufflebottom, Charlie 94, 95
Simpson, Alex 96
Sketrick 24
Smith, Sir Thomas 25
Smuggling 33, 34
Smyth, Canon George 113
Smyth, Gordon 64
Smyth, John 80
Smyth, Mrs 89, 114
Soap making 39
Sparks, Ensign 44
Spence, Noel and Roy 105
Spring dam 51
Square. the 22, 23, 33, 37, 41, 44, 45, 47, 50,
    51, 54, 55, 64, 75, 76, 78, 79, 86, 87, 90,
    93, 95-97, 99-101, 108, 114
St. Mochaoi 20
St. Patrick 19
St. Paul's Cathedral 49
Stapleton, Col. 44
Steele, William 17
Stepping Stones, sheltered housing 103
Stewart, Alexander 37
Stitt, John 41, 50, 56
Stone, Bessie 82, 95; Guy 59, 64

Stones' Plantin' 64
Stone Quarry 40, 58
Strangford Lough 15, 16, 25, 33, 40, 77, 104
Strickland's petrol station 52, 53
Supervalu 38, 69
Swindle, George 66
Swindle, Jim 16

Taggart, Tom 59
Tanner's Row 76
Tannery 76
Taylor, Annabella 45
Taylor, Jeremy, bishop of Down 31
Taylor, Rev. David 113; Taylor's Dam 113
Taylor, W.J. 92
Tennis 69, 70, 92, 93
Thompson, Sam 66
Thompson's hall 41, 68, 94, 95, 108
Tiburon 46
Titanic 84, 85, 99, 103
Todd's Row 96
Toilets 91, 104
Tombstones 27, 52
Tourist Trophy race 67, 68, 97, 98
Tower houses 24, 25
Town Improvement Act 84
Townlands map 110, 111
Traction engines 76
Transport 59, 63-68, 104, 113
Troopersfield 84
Tunnels 57
Twentieth Light Dragoons 46

Ulaid 18
Ulster 15, 18, 22, 28, 30, 37
Ulster Museum 17, 20
Ulster Transport Authority 68
Ulster Volunteer Force 85, 86
Unicarval 43, 99
Unionism 81, 85
Unit, Captain 44
United Irishmen 43, 54

Upper Corn Mill 37, 39, 74, 112
Upper Crescent 95
Uraghamore 41-43, 70, 71

Vellore 48
Victoria Cross 86
Vikings 15, 20, 21
Vincent, Mr. 42
Volunteers 43

War memorial 87
Ward, John 51, 57, 112; Marcus 57, 112
Ward, Paddy 82
Wash mill 39
Watchlights 39
Waterford Loney 52
Watson, Madge 64
Weighbridge 57, 78
Weir Court 103
Wellworth's 105
Wesley, John 42
West Indies 46, 47
Westminster Confession of Faith 32, 61
Whiskey distilling: Lower (Island) Distillery
    51-53, 59, 72, 74, 75, 85, 86, 92, 102; Upper
    (Mound) Distillery 24, 51, 52, 61, 62, 72, 74,
    75, 77, 78, 88-90, 102, 108, 113
White, R.J. (Mickey) 89, 90
Wildfowl and Wetlands Centre 77
William III 32; Williamite Wars 31, 32
Windmill Hill 60, 61
Wishart & Co. 88
Witham, Neil 16
World Wars: First 72, 77, 83, 86; Canadian
    Expeditionary Force 86; Gun in Square 86,
    87, 93; Racecourse Redoubt 86; Somme 82,
    86; 36th Ulster Division 86; Second 72, 87,
    99-101

York Fencibles 43, 44
York Island 44
Young, John 82